God in the Here and Now

And Other Timely Sermons

Elizabeth Dallas McLean

Parson's Porch Books

God in the Here and Now: and Other Timely Sermons
ISBN: Softcover 978-1-946478-05-4
Copyright © 2016 by Elizabeth Dallas McLean

All rights reserved. No part of this book may be reproduced or transmitted in any form or by any means, electronic or mechanical, including photocopying, recording, or by any information storage and retrieval system, without permission in writing from the publisher.

To order additional copies of this book, contact:

Parson's Porch Books

1-423-475-7308

www.parsonsporch.com

Parson's Porch Books is an imprint of Parson's Porch & Company (PP&C) in Cleveland, Tennessee. PP&C is an innovative company which raises money by publishing books of noted authors, representing all genres. All donations from contributors and profits from publishing are shared with the poor.

God in the Here and Now

Contents

Introduction 9

Who You Callin' a Weed? 11
    Matthew 13:24-30; James 4:11-12

A Christian Response to Chicken Little 18
    Jeremiah 32:1-15; 2 Thessalonians 2:16-17

Looking for a King 25
    1 Samuel 8:4-22a; Matthew 25:31-46

Amazing or Offensive Grace? 35
    Jonah 3:1-5, 10-4:4; Matthew 20:1-16

Transformation Triptych 42
    Luke 9:28-43

Sin No More Ash Wednesday 49
    Psalm 51:1-5; John 7:53- 8:11

What Do You See? 53
    Job 19:25-27a; John 20:1-18

The Eternal Now 59
    Ecclesiastes 3:1-8; Matthew 6:25-34

No Cape Required, No Parade Promised 66
    Exodus 1:8-10; 15-21; Luke 10:1-11, 17-20

Christ and the Cosmos: Is Belief in an Immanent God
Compatible with Belief in a Multiverse? 73
    Psalm 8; Colossians 1:15-20

The Way in the World 81
    Amos 9:5-7; John 14:1-7

God on the Go 89
    Genesis 11:27- 12:9; Matthew 8:18-22

According to the Deer of the Dawn 96
    Psalm 22; Lamentations 3:19-24
Divine Metrics.. 104
    Ezekiel 17:22-24; Matthew 13:31-35; 44-46
Gates of Meeting 111
    1 Kings 17:8-24; Luke 7:11-17
Maternal Blessings.. 118
    Isaiah 49: 1, 14-16; Matthew 23:37-39
Once in Woodrow Wilson Service Station.. 126
    A Christmas Eve Homily

To my mother, Jennifer P. McLean, for teaching me how to write, and for loving and supporting me throughout my life and my journey of faith

Introduction

When God called me to leave my law practice to go into ministry, the message I received was that I should be "advocating for the Lord." Up until that point, I had been spending most my time as an environmental litigator advocating for the environment, the law, or for corporations. In the context of the law, I knew what it meant to be "an advocate." It meant standing before a judge or submitting legal briefs speaking on my client's behalf, as well as sitting with clients, and counseling them on their legal obligations so that they would be compliant. But at first I was not at all sure what it meant to be an "advocate for the Lord." Although I was actively involved in a Presbyterian church at the time, I was not at that point evangelical by nature or upbringing. I didn't even know where to begin, and God didn't seem interested in spelling out the particulars. So, twenty years ago, like a good lawyer, I began my journey in seminary so that I could research the needs of my newest client and all the relevant issues. I have spent all my time since then striving to discern with the help of God's best advocate, the Holy Spirit, how best to be fulfill my call.

Over the course of my ministry I have come to recognize that sometimes being an advocate means having to speak prophetically on God's behalf against the ways of the Church or the surrounding culture, however uncomfortable that may be. This is particularly true when the dominant ways of being are unjust, as they so often are. Sometimes being an advocate means that I have had to speak pastorally to people desperately seeking "a word from the Lord" but not able to discern one themselves. There is so much suffering in our world today that even faithful believers need reassuring at times that God does care. In the four churches and one hospital I have served, I have been a caregiver, a teacher, a Christian apologist, a prophet, a story teller, an actor, and, yes, even an evangelist as the circumstances required. But in these roles, there has been a common thread in my message: the Gospel of Jesus Christ is the key, not just to our receiving eternal life with God in heaven one day, but also to our receiving abundant life with God in the here and now. I believe very strongly that Jesus came primarily to tell us that "the Kingdom of God is at hand." He came to enable us to dwell in it now. My job therefore is to help equip people to find it and to fight for it, until that Kingdom is fully visible on earth.

This collection of sermons reflects both my sense of call and the diverse ways I have felt called to fulfill it. Some of the sermons were from a summer series I did called "Faith in the Real World" which was built upon questions submitted by the congregation. They asked, and I tried to answer. But otherwise the sermons are unrelated one to another, inspired by the Lectionary, the newspaper, and the Spirit. They are a cross-section of my attempts to make the Gospel relevant and accessible.

There have been so many servants of God, both ordained and otherwise who have shaped who I am and how I minister that I cannot possibly name and thank them all. But I would like to offer a special word of thanks to the Rev. Dr. Jon Fancher, who enabled me to hear and answer God's call, to the Rev. Dr. Floyd Churn and Rev. Dr. Jim Collier, who helped me to find my voice as a pastor and not as a lawyer, and to Rev. Nancy Lincoln Reynolds, the Rev. Dr. Heather Shortlidge, the Rev. Dr. W. Terry Schoener, Brad Sherrill, and my beloved family whose emotional and spiritual support has been invaluable to me.

Who You Callin' a Weed?
Matthew 13:24-30; James 4:11-12

In the Audrey Hepburn-Cary Grant classic movie *Charade*, no one is who he seems to be. As more and more people are killed off in a life-or-death treasure hunt of sorts, Audrey Hepburn, the only guileless person involved, turns to Cary Grant's character and asks, "Alex, how can you tell if anyone is lying or not?" Grant, whose character's name is not really Alex, responds with a riddle which captures the dilemma upon which the whole movie is based: "There once were two tribes, the Whitefeet and the Blackfeet. The Whitefeet always tell the truth and the Blackfeet always lie. So, one day a man from one of the tribes comes up to you and you say, 'Hey, what are you, a truthful Whitefoot or a lying Blackfoot?" The man responds: 'I am a Truthful Whitefoot.' But which is he really?" "A truthful Whitefoot of course," Hepburn's character responds. "Ah, but why not a lying Blackfoot?" Grant prods. Alarmed and confused, Hepburn responds, "Which one are you?"

It's a great movie, but it's an even greater riddle because it captures so well the dilemma we all face as we go through life: how do you tell the good guys from the bad guys, or in the language of today's parable from *Matthew*, how do you tell the wheat from the tares? The householder's slaves thought they knew the difference; at the very least they could recognize the morning after the householder sowed his seeds that there were weeds in the crop. But the owner was far less confident about their discernment and their skill. He stopped them before they started yanking out the unwanted part of the crop. "Don't pull them now" he said, "because in so doing you will uproot the wheat with them."

In the Middle East, the situation described by the parable was not a farfetched hypothetical. In that region, farmers had a real problem with weeds in the wheat, especially with the particular weed the Greek references in this parable. In the King James Version that weed is called a tare, but in botanical and agricultural circles, it is better known as *lolium temulentum*, also known as darnel or sometimes "cheat."[1] Darnel frequently grew where wheat grew, with disastrous consequences. The problem was not just that fully-grown darnel has a deep and complicated root system which weaves its way in and among the wheat roots making it all but impossible to eradicate, as the householder indicated. It was also that the darnel looks almost identical to wheat (hence the nickname "cheat"), so that you cannot easily pull the weed before the roots get tangled. As you see from your bulletin cover, it is very hard to tell the difference between the wheat and cheat. But for a little black spot on its tip, darnel is virtually indistinguishable from wheat until it is ripe. When the grain is ready, darnel remains upright while wheat bends at the top. But that isn't exactly a helpful distinguishing feature if you are trying to harvest large quantities at once, instead of plucking the grains stem-by-stem.

The intermingling of darnel and wheat was more than a mere nuisance, moreover. It was also a potentially deadly problem because while wheat is great food for most people, (except those like me with gluten sensitivities), darnel is poisonous. If you made and ate a nice loaf of darnel bread, it would taste fine, but soon after you would find yourself nauseated and dizzy, with blurred vision, partial paralysis and worse. The French name for the plant is derived from the French word for drunkenness because of these symptoms. But for animals and people alike, darnel becomes a deadly poison if you eat enough of it. Everyone in Jesus' day knew this, which is why the Romans made it illegal to sow darnel in anyone else's wheat field. Once a regional wheat crop was contaminated, soon everyone would be hard pressed to know what was safe and what was not.

Darnel is not the only poisonous plant to masquerade as something good. Where I lived in Ohio people knew that they had to be very careful about the lovely white wild flowers that bloomed along highways and on the edges of fields and waterways. To uneducated eyes, these flowers looked like beautiful and delicate Queen Anne's lace, perfect for summer bouquets. But often, the white lacy plants were wild hemlock, which is deadly.[2] It was wild hemlock that killed

---

[1] See *Wikipedia, The Free Encyclopedia*, s.v. "Lolium_temulentum," (accessed Aug. G, 2014), https://en.wikipedia.org/wiki/Lolium_temulentum

[2] See e.g. Carson, Angela, "*Poison Hemlock: A Killer Masquerading as a Queen,*" Dave's Garden (June 19, 2012), retrieved from http://davesgarden.com/guides/articles/view/3785 ; or New Life on a

Socrates, and is wild hemlock that still kills many people and animals accidentally today. Children pick the flowers thinking they are beautiful, get the oils on their hands, and then get hideously sick or die. Others die because they eat the root thinking they are eating Queen Anne's lace, which is edible because it is basically wild carrot. One can learn the subtle differences between the two plants to enjoy the flower and avoid the poison. But without education, most people fail to recognize the difference.

You would think, given the risks that these copycat plants cause, that the householder's recommendation in the parable would have been for his slaves to weed very quickly and very carefully. This is the lesson of the parable of the sower. If we want to be good soil, we must weed constantly because otherwise the weeds will choke the Word of God right out of us. But in this parable, which immediately follows the other in *Matthew*, the householder, who stands for God, tells his workers to leave the weeds where they are. "It will all be sorted out later," he says. "So which is it?" you may be asking. "Weed or don't weed?"

The answer is that it depends on who, or what you are calling a weed. The weeds Matthew identified in the sower parable were the love of wealth, and the worries of the world. Like kudzu these weeds can overcome and destroy a person's faith quickly. But in the parable of the wheat and the tares, the weeds aren't objects or emotions, they are people; and that makes all the difference. Jesus wanted his disciples to know two things about people. The first is no surprise: some people are good and some people are not; or more accurately in the context of *Matthew*, some people are faithful and some people are not. But the bad and the wrong in the world are not from God. All that God sows is good. So, when we are frustrated or dismayed by the sin in the world, we must not blame God for it. We must recognize that it is very hard to grow anything good without also growing weeds. Today we might call this lesson the "free will defense." We cannot have the freedom to choose what is right and true and good, without also having the freedom to choose what is wrong and false and bad. We all make good and bad choices because of this freedom, and because we all sin. But Jesus promises that in the end, God's harvest will be all

---

Homestead Blog, "*Wild Carrots, Queen Anne's Lace and Deadly Hemlock*," (June, 2012) retrieved from http://newlifeonahomestead.com/2012/06

good. In the end of time God will rid creation of all that is wrong and false and bad once and for all.

The second and even more important thing we need to know about weedy people is that it is not our business to weed them out while we are waiting for the end of time to come. If we try, we will only end up damaging God's good crop because all of God's plants are interconnected, and because we are not good at distinguishing the weeds from the wheat. We think we are, but we are not.

I heard a wonderful illustration of this truth circulating in the presbytery I belonged to in Ohio years ago.[3] The story goes that on a British Airways flight from Johannesburg, a middle-aged, well-off white South African woman found herself sitting next to a black man. She called the cabin crew attendant over to complain about her seating. "What seems to be the problem, Madam?" asked the attendant. "Can't you see?" she said. "You've sat me next to a (and she used a pejorative racist term I won't repeat). I can't possibly sit next to this disgusting human. Find me another seat!" "Please calm down Madam," the attendant said. "The flight is very full today, but I'll tell you what I'll do. I will go check to see if any seats are available in first class." The woman cocked a snooty look at the outraged black man beside her (not to mention many of the surrounding passengers). A few minutes later the attendant returned with news, which she delivered to the lady who was looking at her neighbors on the plane now with a smug and self-satisfied grin. "Madam, unfortunately, as I suspected, economy class is full. However, we do have one seat left in first class." Before the woman could respond, the attendant continued: "It is most extraordinary to make this kind of upgrade, and I had to get special permission from the captain. But given the circumstances, the captain felt that it was outrageous that someone be forced to sit next to such a person." The attendant then turned to the black man and said, "So, if you'd like to get your things, sir, I have your seat ready for you..." at which point the surrounding

---

[3] I believe the story's original source in the presbytery was a copy of The Muskingum Valley Presbytery Newsletter, 2003. Since preaching this sermon I have learned that the story should be understood as a teaching parable only; the event most likely did not happen. See Mikkleson, David, "Obnoxious Passengers" SNOPES.COM (April, 2012) at
http://www.snopes.com/travel/airline/obnoxious.asp

passengers stood and gave a standing ovation, while the man walked up to the front of the plane."

Throughout the history of humankind, we have used all kinds of invalid criteria to try to identify and separate the tares from the wheat. We have used skin color, gender, economic status, immigration and citizenship status, ethnicity, sexual orientation, education level, nationality, age and religion. We still are. Pick up a paper, and you'll see there isn't enough Ortho weed-be-gone to satisfy either the Israelis or Palestinians these days to heartbreaking and devastating effect. You'll see the cry of "Uproot them or weed them out" being embraced by more groups in Europe against Jews and Muslims alike. In our own country, instead of recognizing the beautiful diverse garden God has given us, more and more people are seeing themselves as flowers and others who differ from them politically or socially as weeds who must be eradicated or the garden will be ruined. And in the Church.... well I'm sorry to say that since it was founded, Christ's disciples seem to have forgotten this parable more than they have followed it, trying to weed out those who are supposedly unfit for the body of Christ. We are yanking and spraying more than ever, and yet all we are succeeding in doing is seriously damaging the whole crop.

If we truly want God's good crop to grow and thrive, we need to let go of the whole idea of "weeds," which is judgmental. A weed, according to the dictionary, is a plant that has been deemed undesirable, unattractive or troublesome. But the term is entirely subjective. Take the dandelion for example. I saw a Facebook post the other day of a dandelion puffball in a child's hand, with the caption that read: "When you look at a field of dandelions, you can either see a hundred weeds or a hundred wishes."[4] It could have just as well said, "or a healing gift from God" however. Did you know that dandelion greens are delicious and good for you? In France, Italy, England and Russia they are a staple in salads for their high nutritional value. Dandelions not only taste good, they also have well-established medicinal benefits including providing relief for stomach, gall bladder and liver problems; and as annoying as they may seem to be when they pop up all over your lawn, they are good for your soil because the same deep tap root which frustrates

---

[4] Internet Meme, Facebook, www.facebook.com, retrieved 8-2-14.

weeders pulls up needed minerals into the decalcified soil in which dandelions tend to grow.

Even wild hemlock has an upside, as it turns out. Yes, it is an extremely poisonous plant, but when used carefully in small quantities by those who know what they are doing, it has proven to have many beneficial qualities in medicines. The fact that the poison attacks the nervous system has allowed it to be used therapeutically in remedies for breathing problems including bronchitis, whooping cough, and asthma; and for painful conditions including teething in children, swollen and painful joints, and cramps.

The more we obsess with trying to rid ourselves, our Church and our society of perceived undesirables, the more we risk both damaging God's good crop and becoming like insidious weeds ourselves. This is because the same hatred and pride, sin and selfishness which we do not want around, the same Sin with a capital S, grows within our hearts every time we categorize others as undesirables, instead of seeing them as imperfect but beloved children of God like ourselves. These negative feeling poison the grace and love God has planted within us. Maybe that is why Jesus chose darnel for the illustration in his parable. The plant is not actually poisonous innately; it is made that way by a deadly fungus that grows on its seeds. Remove the fungus, and maybe we'd all enjoy darnel bread sandwiches. Likewise, if we spent more time trying to eradicate the fungus of judgmentalism, which contaminates human hearts and leads to deadly dehumanizing attitudes and practices in the world, instead of trying to label weeds, then there would be a whole lot less poison available to harm both the wheat and the weeds in God's crop.

In many Native American languages, there is no such word as weed because the tribes do not believe it is their place to judge the value of what God has created. So, they have words like dandelion and darnel, but not weed or pest. Native American culture recognizes that there is good and bad in everything and everyone. It does not deny the reality of the bad in people and the world. But it also recognizes that what may be unpleasant or undesirable to one, may be good and desirable for another. The message of the Bible is not much different from this. The Gospel affirms that we all have both sin and goodness within us, just as there is both good and evil in the world. We all are potentially wheat and potentially tare. As disciples of Christ, therefore, it is not our job to weed out others, but to weed ourselves of the worry and greed, the hatred and pride, the judgmentalism and fear which chokes the Word of God our divine Sower so extravagantly sowed within us.

Thanks be to God for having the graciousness to sow so wildly, the patience to allow us all to grow into greater fruitfulness, and the wisdom to entangle us together, so that through the abundant mercy of God, there will be that much more love to harvest in the end. Amen

A Christian Response to Chicken Little
Jeremiah 32:1-15; 2 Thessalonians 2:16-17

Last week before I left for my weekend off, a cousin of mine posted an editorial from the *New York Times* on Facebook called *"The Great Unraveling"* by Roger Cohen.[5] The editorial prompted a lot of discussion among my friends, as well as 1,200 comments to the newspaper because it tapped into an unspoken anxiety and disease that I think many people, including myself at times, are feeling these days about the state of the world and our prospects for the future. Most of my friends were disturbed and depressed by the editorial; most of the comments to the *Times* were depressed and angry political comments assigning blame for the state of affairs to various leaders. But what I found lacking and desperately needed among the responses was a Christian response. There was no response which offered good news. So today I want to do something a little different. I am going to respond to the editorial here, not to promote Cohen, whom I know nothing about, nor the *Times*, which I rarely read. I am doing this because I think that we all as Christians need to be clear in our hearts, minds and souls that by the grace of the God we know in Jesus Christ, there is an alternative perspective to the common world view that Cohen articulates. There is also a better response to the bad news of today than blaming politicians, wringing our hands, or hunkering down to wait for the apocalypse with a few six packs or gallons of Ben & Jerry's. That response, the Christian response, is one which articulates and encourages hope. It is one that we are called to proclaim and promote.

So here is an edited-for-length version of Cohen's editorial *"The Great Unraveling"*[6]

---

[5] Cohen, Roger, *"The Great Unraveling"* NEW YORK TIMES (Sept. 16, 2014) Opinion Section, retrieved from http://www.nytimes.com/2014/09/16/opinion/roger-cohen-the-great-unraveling.html (©NY Times; used with permission.)
[6] *Ibid.*

It was the time of unraveling. Long afterward, in the ruins, people asked: How could it happen?

It was a time of beheadings. With a left-handed sawing motion, against a desert backdrop, in bright sunlight, a Muslim with a British accent cut off the heads of two American journalists and a British aid worker. The jihadi seemed comfortable in his work, unhurried. His victims were broken. Terror is theater....

It was a time of aggression. The leader of the largest nation on earth pronounced his country encircled, even humiliated. He annexed part of a neighboring country, the first such act in Europe since 1945, and stirred up a war on further land he coveted. His surrogates shot down a civilian passenger plane. The victims, many of them Europeans, were left to rot in the sun for days. He denied any part in the violence, like a puppeteer denying that his puppets' movements have any connection to his. He invoked the law the better to trample on it. He invoked history the better to turn it into farce...

It was a time of weakness. The most powerful nation on earth was tired of far-flung wars, its will and treasury depleted by absence of victory. An ungrateful world could damn well police itself. The nation had bridges to build and education systems to fix. Civil wars between Arabs could fester. Enemies might even kill other enemies, a low-cost gain. Middle Eastern borders could fade; they were artificial colonial lines on a map. Shiite could battle Sunni, and Sunni Shiite, there was no stopping them. Like Europe's decades-long religious wars, these wars had to run their course. The nation's leader mockingly derided his own "wan, diffident, professorial" approach to the world, implying he was none of these things, even if he gave that appearance. He set objectives for which he had no plan.... [T]he world was already adrift, unmoored by the retreat of its ordering power. The rule book had been ripped up.

It was a time of hatred. Anti-Semitic slogans were heard in the land that invented industrialized mass murder for Europe's Jews. Frightened European Jews removed mezuzahs from their homes. Europe's Muslims felt the ugly backlash from the depravity of the decapitators, who were adept at Facebooking their message. The fabric of society frayed. Democracy looked quaint or outmoded beside new authoritarianisms. Politicians, haunted by their incapacity, played on the fears of their populations, who were device-distracted or under device-driven stress.... The great rising nations of vast populations held the fate of the world in their hands but hardly seemed to care.

It was a time of fever. People in West Africa bled from the eyes.

It was a time of disorientation. Nobody connected the dots... [u]ntil it was too late and people could see the Great Unraveling for what it was and what it had wrought.

Cheery stuff isn't it? We can dismiss it quickly, as one reader did, with the response, "It was the time of melodrama," or join others in pointing fingers at the politicians or the political parties we think are causing the problems Cohen names. We can hunker down and brace ourselves for World War III or the global apocalypse that Cohen clearly thinks is coming, making sure that we have a year's worth of supplies to take care of our own families like the Mormons do. We can despair. But according to the Bible, these are not the most faithful of responses. The most faithful thing we can do is to reject despair and instead strive to live into future with hope that God promised first to the Israelites through Jeremiah, and then ultimately to the world through Christ. We can nurture with hope, plan with hope, and encourage others to do so as well.

The hope of the Bible is not some kind of naive optimism which invites us to sing, "Always look on the bright side of life," while hanging on a cross, like the main character does in the Monty Python classic, *"Life of Brian."* That kind of optimism requires ignoring reality. It doesn't solve anything, change anything, or sustain anyone engaged in the world for very long. No, the hope of the Bible is a perspective which is deeply grounded. But it is a reality which is not limited to the sum of all the awful and depressing events and situations in our world, however. These are only part of the picture. The other part of the picture is defined by the larger reality of the God who is faithful to divine promises, who has demonstrated the power to work good out of even the most horrible bad, and who in Jesus Christ gave us a light so bright and transforming that even the world's greatest darkness and death itself could not defeat it. In other words, Christian hope, as author Paul Zahl put it, is grounded in "remembrance projected onto the future. It satisfies because it is based on an objective past."[7] God has worked amazing good out of a whole host of horrible circumstances in the past. And even now God is at work in our world doing the same.

---

[7] Miller, The Rev. Neale L., *"Beyond Recognition,"* delivered at Lakeview Presbyterian Church, retrieved from
http://www.lpcno.org/beyondrecognition.html

Consider the past we heard about in today's Old Testament lesson for example. It's hard for us to imagine just how bleak things were for Jeremiah and the people of Judah when this text takes place. The northern kingdom of Israel had long since fallen to the Assyrian Empire, and now the Southern Kingdom of Judah was all but destroyed by the Babylonians. This was disaster for the Jews on an apocalyptic scale. There was little food or water. All the land around Jerusalem had been captured or burned into a wasteland, including Jeremiah's hometown of Anathoth, about three miles outside of the city. Most of the Israelites had already been killed, raped, or taken into slavery. And as if that weren't bad enough, Jeremiah was stuck waiting for the end of it all from a prison cell in Jerusalem because the king of Judah had not liked his prophecy that Babylon would conquer the city.

If ever there was a time when the majority would agree that the end was near, it was that time. But during the darkness and the fear, the word of the Lord came to Jeremiah in his prison cell and told him to do something extraordinary. "Go buy your cousin's land in Anathoth" God said. This wasn't divine insider trading tip: buy low now and sell high later. The land God was talking about was already in Babylonian hands. Jeremiah wasn't going to be able to sell it to anyone, or to live there any time soon. But God insisted, "Buy the land now. File the deeds publicly. Let it be made known that even from behind prison bars you have reason to hope from what you know of God, and that others have reason to hope as well." So, Jeremiah bought his cousin's land. He followed all the rules of the Mosaic covenant about registering the deed and announcing the purchase publicly. Then the deed was put away safely in a clay jar (much like the Dead Sea scrolls centuries later), where it would be safe until Jeremiah's descendants could resettle the land and rebuild.

Jeremiah's act of spending his last dime from prison on a bit of prophetic performance art did two things. First, it showed the people of Judah that Jeremiah was willing to put his money where his mouth was when it came to his prophecies. He wasn't just making this stuff up. He trusted in God with his heart, mind, soul and strength, even when he was in prison, even when the sky was falling on the people of Judah, and Jerusalem was all but lost. So, if God said that the exile would not be the end of the people, that in time they would return and can rebuild, then Jeremiah believed God. And he wanted others to as well.

The other thing Jeremiah's buying the land did was give his cousin the ability to hope too. Hanamel had nothing. The reason he came to Jeremiah in prison is that Jeremiah was his last hope. Hanamel was going to lose the family land; he was struggling to survive. So, Jeremiah's act of buying his land equipped his cousin both financially and spiritually to hope himself.

In a nutshell, this is what we Christians are called to do. We are called to ground our hope in God even during darkness and suffering, and we are called to share that hope with others by pointing to the possibilities for change, and by investing ourselves emotionally, spiritually and concretely in God's vision of the future, not the world's apocalyptic vision. Our knowledge of and faith in God give us reason to hope when others have given up. And then, as we will affirm in a little bit with the *Declaration of Faith, 1977*, our "hope gives us courage for the struggle." It allows us to see the world in terms of grace and new life, instead of seeing it only through the lens of fear and loss. Once we can do that, the world, even in its serious brokenness, is rich with possibilities and promise.

If we were to write an editorial about the world today from the perspective of Christian hope instead of Cohen's gloom and doom, right here and right now, notwithstanding the world's great brokenness, it could sound something like this: "It was a time of great potential, and great hope. It was a time of unprecedented breakthroughs in medical treatment and healing. New gene therapies were cheating death by eradicating even stage four cancers from people's bodies with minimal side effects. Robotics was giving limbs and movement back to the injured. New scientific research was discovering the mechanisms which caused ALS, Parkinson's and Alzheimer's, so that cures for these terrible diseases seemed well within reach soon, and HIV was being transformed from a death sentence into a manageable disease. It was a time of growing connectedness. The Internet was allowing individuals and nations to know of the needs of people on the opposite side of the globe, opening doors to sharing resources, skills and more. Cell phones were breaking down barriers of isolation caused by the lack of land lines in remote or poor villages. As our nations grew more and more diverse, we were learning more about each other, and experiencing unprecedented opportunities to build community which transcends geography, nationality, gender and age. Shared technology and education was strengthening development and increasing employment worldwide. It was a time of resource development and reallocation. Although gross economic inequality was still a problem, one billion people were taken out of extreme poverty in half the time the powerful nations of the world allotted for the task. Solar energy became more common and cost-sustainable; hybrid car use reduced our dependence on fossil fuels further; and 3-D printing was just beginning to take off, demonstrating that it would be possible to find new ways to protect the environment, preserve resources, and maybe even provide organs to those in need."

You could write a similar editorial of your own life as well. Instead of focusing on the people who have left you or died, the jobs you have lost or left, the weight you have gained, the health issues you have developed, the wrongs that have been done to you, or your anger at the way things are, allow the healing and hopeful love of God to fill your heart and mind, put your trust in God's power to transform, and you will start to see how blessed you are. You will see the people in your life, the opportunities to learn and use new gifts, the access to unsurpassed medical care and more. Hope doesn't erase the problems, but it does let you see beyond them.

Thornton Wilder once said, "Hope is a projection of the imagination; so is despair. Despair all too readily embraces the ills it foresees; hope is an energy and arouses the mind to explore every possibility to combat them... In response to hope the imagination is aroused to picture every possible issue, to try every door, to fit together even the most heterogeneous pieces in the puzzle."[8] When we ground ourselves in the reality of the faithfulness of God, the sustaining love of God, and God's power to transform, the hope our imagination projects is not pie-in-the-sky fantasy. It is imminently practical. It acknowledges all the problems in the world, but also acknowledges that with God's help, if we invest our energy and our emotional well-being in discerning and nurturing the kingdom-

---

[8] Peterson, Eugene H., A Long Obedience in the Same Direction: Discipleship in an Instant Society (Downers Grove: InterVarsity Press, 2000), 136.

values of healing, reconciliation, love and peace, we have every reason to be hopeful for our future because God has already shown us that God's ability to redeem and to rebirth is greater than our ability to enslave and destroy.

In 1890, Dr. Charles Sheldon, a 43-year old pastor of Topeka's Central Congregational Church, took over editing the *Topeka Capital* for one week on a dare from its publisher.[9] Sheldon had preached a story about a newspaper which pledged to deliver the news only as Jesus would have it do. The publisher thought the paper would die if it was ever run that way, so he gave Sheldon a week to prove him wrong. Sheldon did as he wanted to, printing the Sermon on the Mount on the front page, and focusing on feel-good stories and helping the poor, instead of violence, sex, gossip and crime. In the week that Sheldon ran his newspaper, circulation went from 11,223 to 362,000, with copies sold as far from Kansas as the Boer Republic in South Africa. People have always needed reason to hope. But when Sheldon's week was up, the *New York Herald* panned his efforts by saying he had left out all the important news for the week, the plagues, the fires, the wars, and the death of a boxing champ. So, no one agreed on who won the bet.[10]

I'm not in favor of leaving out all the sad and horrible news. We need to know what is going on in the world in order to help our neighbors. But as Christians, every day in our own lives, in our conversations with others, and in the world, we can respond to the bad news with the equally good news that God is at work in our midst, and is even now showing us the way to the future with hope we all desire. We have been given comfort and good hope through the love and grace of God in Jesus Christ, as *Second Thessalonians* reminds us. And that makes us, as Paul told the Corinthians, clay jars which hold the treasure of God on which our hope is based. In our words and in our actions, therefore, let us be instruments of hope and not despair; let us trust and invest in the Lord. Amen.

---

[9] Anderson, Phil, "*Sheldon's Message Was Simple*," THE TOPEKA CAPITAL JOURNAL ONLINE, posted 2:05 a.m. on Sunday, March 12, 2000, retrieved Sept. 22, 2014 from
http://cjonline.com/indepth/sheldon/stories/031200_sheldonmsg.shtml

[10] Hughes, Ina, A Sense of Human (Knoxville: The Knoxville News-Sentinel Co., 1993), 179-181.

Looking for a King
1 Samuel 8:4-22a; Matthew 25:31-46

A few hundred years after the people of Israel moved into the Promised Land, Samuel, who was then acting as God's chosen judge and prophet, came to God and said, "God, we've got a problem." The problem was that the people no longer wanted to live as a theocracy, a nation ruled by God as their invisible king with human "judges" as God's helpers. The people wanted a normal kind of visible human king. Like children envying the toys of their classmates, the people had come to Samuel and said the equivalent of "We want a king like the other nations have. We want the kind that comes with a palace and an army and power and riches and fame. We want a king we can see, and one that the other nations will know and fear." When Samuel told God about the people's request, God shook God's head and said, "A human king isn't going to be good for them. Go tell them that a human king will sacrifice their sons to his wars, and take their daughters to be his servants. He will tax them oppressively and take their land and a big chunk of their herds and their crops. He won't listen to the needs of the people or care for them the way I do." So, Samuel relayed God's words to the people. "We don't care what you say. We still want a human king like all the other nations have" the people cried. So, God threw up God's hands and said, "Ok, I'll give you what you wish for. But don't say I didn't warn you."

Years later, when the people were in exile in Babylon in large part because of the bad choices and practices of their human kings, some of them looked back on this moment and thought, "Oh, now we get it. We should have stayed with our invisible God as king. But even then, there were still some who thought, "No, we just need to find the right human king and it will all work out." So, the two books of *Samuel* depict the monarchy as the beginning of the end of the people of Israel, and the two books of *Chronicles* depict the monarchy as a good thing that just had some kinks to be worked out. Ever since then Jewish theology has been ambivalent about kings.

Many Christians are just as ambivalent. As American lovers of democracy, we don't want a king to rule our nation; we don't want anyone who has that kind of power to take, or to tell us what to do.

But as people of faith, we still struggle with the invisibility of our God. Even though we affirm today on the liturgical calendar that Christ is our King, many of us don't know what it means that he is our king. It's hard to follow and serve someone you have not physically seen or heard. Before we can recognize his kingship, we must feel as though we recognize him, as though we know him; and many Christians don't feel that they do. They want to, and search for Jesus all their lives. But they are never sure that they truly find him. Other Christians think they know Christ but the Christ they know is not always the Jesus of the Bible. So today I would like us to consider who Jesus is to us, and who we wish he would be. It's important to ask both questions, because as Albert Schweitzer observed, most people who go looking for Christ inevitably end up finding someone who has been made in their image of who Christ was, rather than a mystery made in the image of God.[11]

Author, historian and religion professor, Stephen Prothero has written a fascinating book about the many ways Jesus has been imagined and re-imagined in American culture according to the cultural stereotypes and wishes of the people.[12] As this Currier & Ives print from the 19th Century illustrates, for quite a while, Jesus was perceived as effeminate because of his unwillingness to claim and use power in traditionally masculine ways.

---

[11] See Schweitzer, Albert, The Quest for the Historical Jesus a Critical Study of its Progress from Reimarus to Wrede, W. Montgomery Trans. (London: Adam and Charles Black, 1910); Wikipedia, The Free Encyclopedia, s.v. "The Quest of the Historical Jesus," (accessed Nov. 11, 2014), https://en.wikipedia.org/wiki/TheQuestoftheHistoricalJesus

[12] Prothero, Stephen, American Jesus: How the Son of God Became a National Icon (New York: Farrar, Strauss and Giroux, 2003).

God in the Here and Now

Currier & Ives print *El Señor, Andando Sobre el Mar*

A lover of children and practitioner of radical forgiveness, Jesus was envisioned as gentle, meek and mild, and therefore, in the eyes of many, was considered weak. But in the early 20th Century, a movement began championed by someone named the Reverend Bruce Barton, to change the way that Jesus was understood and depict him more like a "normal" kind of admirable American leader instead. The result: someone I like to call CEO Jesus.

Clifford S. Davis' painting, *"The Conformist"*[13]

The CEO Jesus was classically manly, confident and business-oriented. CEO Jesus was in favor of capitalism and knew the secret to material prosperity and success. He was the boss of the Church, which was best run like a business. Clifford Davis called his painting of CEO Jesus *"The Conformist"* reflecting the fact that this image, which so many people have of Jesus whether they imagine him in a suit or not, is one in which Jesus' Gospel message largely conforms with American ideals and values about strength, wisdom, manliness, leadership, and success.

---

[13] Clifford S. Davis, "The Conformist", 1993, 20" x 16" alkyd on canvas, Private Collection. © Clifford S. Davis 1993. (Used with permission.)

God in the Here and Now

Stephen Sawyer's "*Undefeated*"[14]

Speaking of manliness, check out this painting by Stephen Sawyer, which attempted to add more muscle both to Jesus and to Christianity by depicting him as someone who looks to me like the creepy love child of Fabio and Hulk Hogan. Sawyer called his painting, "*Undefeated.*" I bet the people in Samuel's day would have liked someone like this for their king. He looks like he could have easily taken on the Goliaths of their age. This image is the exact opposite of the classical image of the suffering Jesus of the cross. This Jesus is a strong and powerful conqueror and winner, someone who inspires confidence for people who admire strength as power.

Some people imagine Jesus not as strong, however, but as otherworldly. Their Jesus is more like this painting by Salvador Dali[15],

---

[14] Stephen S. Sawyer, "Undefeated", © Stephen S. Sawyer, 1999 (used with permission). See www.ART4GOD.com

[15] Salvador Dali, "The Last Supper" (detail), The National Gallery © Salvador Dalí, Fundació Gala-Salvador Dalí, Artists Rights Society (ARS), New York 2016 (used with permission); The Art Archive at Art Resource, NY.

The Last Supper **by Salvador Dali**

which in my opinion is just as disturbing as the macho Fabio Jesus is. This Jesus combines youth with a kind of New Age spiritual guru-vibe that speaks to people who are seeking a wise sage or magical wizard, not a challenging Jewish prophet or a macho king.

This last image was born of science, as well as speculation and imagination. Years ago, a forensic anthropologist named Richard Neaves used classic forensic techniques to "create the face" that may have gone with a 1st Century scull. Someone saw that image and then later used digital technology to enhance the picture of that scull to make it look even more realistic. *Popular Mechanics* then picked up the image and ran an article suggesting that the picture might suggest what Jesus had looked like since he was a 1st Century Galilean male.[16] The picture is not really a digital or forensic creation of what Jesus looked like. No one claims to have found Jesus' scull. But the picture does help to remind us that the real Jesus probably looked nothing

---

[16] Filton, Mike, "*The Real Face of Jesus*," POPULAR MECHANICS, Dec. 7, 2002, retrievable at
http://www.popularmechanics.com/science/health/forensics/1282186.

like the other pictures we've seen, not just because of how they characterize him, but also because they all imagine Jesus as a Caucasian person. He wasn't.

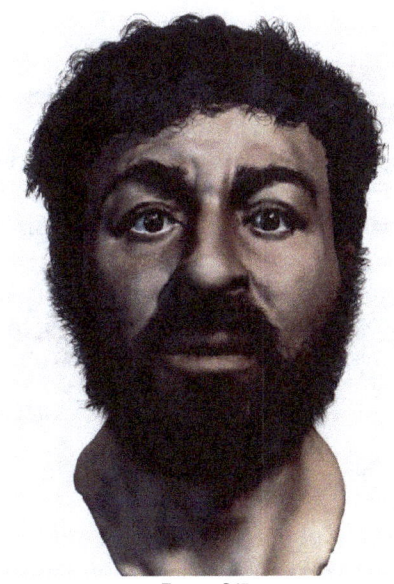

Jesus?[17]

He looked like a typical Middle Eastern man, not extra tall or extra muscular, not glowing with a visible halo. Of course, the forensic face would be more compelling if they had added a little life into it. If he had a twinkle in his eye, or a look of divine love, or even the passion of prophetic outrage in his expression, he might look a little more Christ-like to us. But the point is that Jesus looked so unremarkable and ordinary that when it came time for Judas to betray him, the Romans needed Judas to point him out from among the disciples. The soldiers didn't recognize him on their own.

Neither the sheep nor the goats recognized him in Jesus' parable in *Matthew* today either. It isn't a real parable; it is more like an

---

[17] "Reconstruction of the Face of Jesus"; photographer Bob Collier/Sygma /Getty Images (©Gettyimages. Used with permission.)

apocalyptic drama depicting what Matthew envisioned would happen at the end of time. But in this familiar story, neither the sheep who have been caring for the hungry and the thirsty, the homeless and the imprisoned, nor the goats, who have not been caring for all of them recognized that they were in the presence of "the king." "Gosh, Lord," the goats say, "if we had known they were you, we would have done something." And the sheep say, "When did we see you hungry, thirsty, naked or in prison again? We don't remember seeing you."

There is a lot about this lesson which is troubling because it is about divine judgment. I much prefer to preach on the inclusive texts in the Bible than the judgment texts– that's my own Jesus bias. And we could devote a whole morning to unpacking whether this story came from Jesus or Matthew, and was intended for everyone or just for the Gentiles. But for today, I just want to point out that during the judging and sorting, there is encouragement in this lesson in the fact that no one recognizes Jesus, neither the faithful nor the unfaithful.

What matters in this story is not whether you feel you have seen or know Jesus. What matters is whether you do as he commanded we do: love your neighbor as yourself. This seems to suggest that if we want to find Jesus, instead of trying to find someone who fits our image, or remaking Jesus into it, we would do better to allow him to remake us into his so that we can live like him. We need to strive to live as residents of his kingdom instead of turning him into an acceptable king in our world. Behavior flows from belief. We all can dwell in Jesus' kingdom even if we feel we have never recognized the king. We just need to accept his definitions of what is weak and what is strong, what is wise and what is foolish, what is valuable and what is valueless instead of our own, drawing from all we know of Christ in Scripture. If we do, our behavior will follow.

This is hard because Jesus' definitions, and Jesus' way is not our way. If we want to dwell in the kingdom of God, we must set aside our image of Jesus and embrace instead the Jesus we can know from Scripture. That Jesus does embody many of the qualities we value. He is powerful and confident; he is other-worldly and wise. He knows the secret to success, and he is undefeatable. Yet this Jesus is also compassionate and loving, he is vulnerable and merciful. He is unfailingly just, and consistently self-giving. We can learn from each of these qualities how to live his way. Historical Jesus scholar Marcus Borg put it this way. He said "The image of Jesus.... confronts us at many points. As a charismatic, Jesus is a vivid challenge to our notion of reality, the 'practical atheism' of much of our culture and church. As a sage, he calls us to leave the life of conventional wisdom, whether secular or religious, American or Christian.... As a renewal movement founder and prophet, he points us to human community and history, to an alternative culture which seeks to make the world more compassionate."[18]

When we choose Jesus' ways and definitions over our own and over the world's ways and definitions, regardless of what our mental image is of Jesus' appearance, we are essentially choosing for Jesus to be our king. He isn't a king in the classic human sense. He doesn't come with a visible palace or crown, or even the power to intimidate the nations any more. But he is our king nevertheless. When we choose to live as he lived, moreover, we become as the sheep in the parable, and we receive the assurance that even though our king is invisible, he is with us.

This is the most wonderful and unexpected part of the whole business. When we stop trying to find Jesus, and instead strive to follow him, we can't go two feet without tripping over him because Jesus is present in every vulnerable person we help, in every rally for justice, in every moment of prayer and ministry of compassion. We can't see him, at least not in the traditional sense. But when we remember from Matthew's parable that he is with us; we can see him in a different way.

Seminary professor Peter Gathje discovered this when he was volunteering at a shelter for homeless addicts in Memphis. He volunteered three mornings a week, and had been frustrated for six months by a homeless mentally ill crack addict named Henry Lee, who was obnoxious, loud, and pushy most of the time. But one slow morning, everything changed when he asked Henry Lee what his favorite song was. Suddenly Henry began to smile and started belting out the old Bill Withers' classic, "*Lean on Me.*" With horrible voice and pure joy Henry sang, "Sometimes in our lives, we all have pain, we all have sorrow. But if we are wise, we know that there's always

---

[18] Borg, Marcus J., Jesus A New Vision: Spirit, Culture, and The Life of Discipleship (New York: HarperSanFrancisco, 1987), 199.

tomorrow. Lean on me, when you're not strong, and I'll be your friend. I'll help you carry on, for it won't be long 'til I'm gonna need somebody to lean on." Before he knew what he was doing, Peter found himself joining in with Henry. And then another homeless addict named Linda, who hadn't said a word or smiled in months, also joined in on the line "I just might have a problem that you'd understand. We all need somebody to lean on." In that moment, Peter wept with joy. Writing about the experience later, he said that he felt he had "tasted something of God's kingdom: black, white, housed and homeless, supposedly sane and supposedly mentally ill, addicts and prostitutes and a seminary professor all bound together in a place where God welcomes everyone notwithstanding brokenness, sinfulness and shortcomings. We all need someone to lean on. We all need God's redeeming grace. When the song ended, I could no longer look at Henry Lee or Linda Faye in the same way. They became redemptive for me; they had become the very presence of Jesus and his love in my life."[19]

May we all dwell in God's kingdom not just this day but every day; and in so doing, may we recognize the very presence of the only king we need. Amen.

---

[19] Gathje, Peter R., *"The Cross and the Resurrection in Serving the Poor,"* in THE LIVING PULPIT, Vol. 17, No. 1, Jan.- Mar. 2008, 17. (Used with permission.)

Amazing or Offensive Grace?

Jonah 3:1-5, 10-4:4; Matthew 20:1-16

Imagine that somebody presents you with $100. It isn't an outright gift, however; there are some strings attached. You can keep some of the money, but if you want any of it, you first must agree with an anonymous person how you will divide the sum. The rules are strict. The two of you are in separate rooms and cannot exchange information about yourselves or your circumstances. Additionally, you can make only a single offer of how to split the sum with the other person, who can answer yes or no only, not make a counter offer. The responder knows that the potential pot is $100. If he or she answers "yes" to what you offer, the deal goes forward and you both get your money. If he or she answers "no" then neither of you gets anything. The game is over as soon as the responder responds. What will you offer? Before you form your mental answer keep in mind that it is always in the best interest of the responder to take the money, even if what is offered is only $1. That's still one dollar more than the person had before, even if the other person does end up with $99. So how much would you offer?

Although logic dictates that the people who get to make the offer can keep most of the money if they offer just enough to make the other person accept the deal; and although logic also dictates that the people offered the deal should always accept it no matter how small the sum, as it turns out, real people do not behave logically when they play the Ultimatum Game, as this exercise is called by economists. When real people play this game, two thirds of them offer close to 50%, and more than half of them also reject offers if they are less than 20%.[20] Why? Participants do this because as it turns out, when it comes to the distribution of resources in situation like this where all things are otherwise equal, real people are not motivated primarily by objective logic, sound financial planning or even basic math; they are motivated primarily by their own subjective understandings of fairness. It doesn't seem fair to offer much less than

---

[20] Sigmund, Karl, Fehr, Ernst, and Nowak, Martin A., "*The Economics of Fair Play*," SCIENTIFIC AMERICAN, Jan. 2002: 83-87.

50%, nor does it seem fair to have to accept a pittance when the other guy gets a windfall. While the specific sums offered and accepted varied a bit in some tribes whose understanding of gift-giving differs significantly from Western culture's understanding, the study demonstrated that fairness was a critical variable in the game for human beings all around the world.

Given this, it is not at all surprising that most people, even faithful people, have real problems with Jesus' parable about the vineyard owner and his laborers. Even though everyone ends up with some money in the end, the whole arrangement seems patently unfair. The laborers who work all day in the hot sun get paid the same amount as the workers who put in only an hour at the end of the day. If the late comers worked 90% less than the day laborer, then they shouldn't they be paid 90% less? Even young children think so. So, if our God is supposed to be a God of justice and righteousness, then where is the justice in this parable? For that matter, where is the wisdom in Jesus' teaching this kind of lesson about the kingdom of heaven either? If Jesus was talking about getting into heaven, then such a story provides little incentive for people to work toward that reward, given that apparently you can have fun most of your life and still get in just the same at the end. And if Jesus was talking about the kingdom of God on earth, the story doesn't exactly make that kingdom sound appealing. Life on earth is unfair enough already. Who wants to strive to dwell in God's kingdom on earth if it is still unfair?

Christians have never liked this parable, especially Protestant American Christians like us who were raised with a strong work ethic. So, in order to make the parable more palatable, almost from the very beginning, biblical scholars have argued that this must be an allegorical lesson, not a lesson on what good labor practices should be. This is an allegory about Jews and Gentiles and how they will all receive salvation. The Jews who had been working for God for a long time would get their reward in heaven. The Gentiles, who were comparatively late to the party, would also get their reward through Jesus Christ. In other words, this is just a little story Jesus told to prepare his Jewish listeners for what was going to happen through his death and resurrection. The God who was always just to the Jews was now going to be generous to the Gentiles as well.

This allegorical approach to the text does make it feel a little less offensive, especially when you consider that we are the descendants of the Gentiles in the story. But as uncomfortable and challenging as this parable is, I am still not convinced that we should let ourselves completely off the hook by telling ourselves that the story is little more than a salvation history lesson in disguise. What if this parable is not just about God's grand plan for humankind's salvation? The last few verses seem to suggest that this vineyard story has at least as much to teach us about human "sour grapes" as it does about God's plans for salvation. "Am I not allowed to do what I choose with what belongs to me?" the vineyard owner asks. "Or are you envious because I am generous?" There's the rub! The day laborers did get paid exactly what they were contractually promised. That's justice. The problem is not that they were cheated or paid less than a day's living wage. The problem is that the late workers were paid the same amount despite working less. The problem is the vineyard owner was generous. That's not injustice, that's grace.

Have you heard the expression, "Justice is getting what we deserve. Mercy is *not* getting what we deserve. Grace is getting *better* than we deserve?"[21] This parable affirms the outlandish, even offensive, yet amazing graciousness of God. God gives us what we need even when we don't deserve it because God has the ability, the love and the desire to do so. Grace is the currency of the kingdom of God. "Go ahead and take the $100," God says in the Ultimatum Game. "You need it more than I do." We all are recipients of God's generous grace because we are all sinners. But those of us who strive hard to do the right thing and live faithful lives can sometimes forget that God has given us this grace as a generous gift. We can convince ourselves that we receive saving grace as payment for our faithfulness or our labor. So, when we see God being generous with someone we feel has not earned the grace as we have, instead of seeing a reflection of ourselves in them and giving thanks for what we have also received, we feel that our work has now been devalued, and find ourselves wanting to give them the stink eye in our minds and hearts. "Is your eye evil because I am good?" the vineyard owner asks in the Greek, making it very clear

---

[21] Beeson, Ray, <u>That I May Know Him</u> (Old Tappan: Fleming H. Revell, 1990), 37.

that God knows exactly how these situations make human beings, even good ones, feel.

We aren't the first to feel this way. God was well-acquainted with Jonah's evil eye as well. Jonah did not want to go to warn the Ninevites of their pending destruction; and with good reason. Nineveh was the capital of the Assyrian Empire, the very same empire which threatened the lives of the people of the Northern Kingdom of Israel, and ultimately destroyed that kingdom in 722 B.C.E. The people of Nineveh were "enemy number one" as far as Jonah was concerned. So, the last thing he wanted to do was go into the heart of enemy territory to deliver a message the enemy would not want to hear. But after the embarrassing and very scary fish incident, Jonah did just this. "God's going to destroy you in 40 days," he preached, probably with a little more joy in his voice than was wise. Miraculously, the people listened to him anyway. Today seminary students are told that if one person says that your sermon spoke to them on a Sunday morning then the sermon that week was a success. But in Jonah's case, the whole city responded, including the animals, covering themselves in sack cloth and praying that God would spare them. Talk about a success story! Their repentance impressed God so much that God did spare them. But instead of Jonah feeling good about this turn of events, that his work has spared the lives of thousands, he sat under a bush glaring at the city with such an evil eye that regardless of their repentance, he would have zapped the Ninevites on the spot himself if only he could have.

"You are always so gracious and merciful and abounding in steadfast love." "Are you actually saying that's a bad thing?" God responded. "What right do you have to be angry, you who just a few days ago disobeyed me so badly that you had to be swallowed whole by a fish to learn your lesson?" What right do we have to be angry if God loves people we find to be unlovable, or forgives people we find to be unforgivable? What right do we have to be envious if God blesses those we find undeserving? We have that right only if God made it clear to us that our receiving divine love and mercy, generosity and blessing was contingent upon our good behavior and labor. But God has said just the opposite through Jesus Christ. In Christ God has said, "I will love you even though you are broken. I will love you even though you sin. I will shower you in redeeming grace because

I want to and can, not because you deserve it and not even because you try to earn it."

Do we want to shout, "Unfair!" to such generous grace? Do we want a God who offers only merit-based scholarships to get into the kingdom of heaven? Some people still say "yes." They say that if our work or our faithfulness does not decide our fate then God is discounting our value and offering nothing but cheap grace. There is no reason to strive to be good then. But besides the fact that this argument falsely assumes that something can have value only if we earn it, this perspective also assumes that grace is nothing but a golden ticket into heaven. It is far more than that. God's grace is what we need to live to the fullest in this life. God's grace is the reason we can have a relationship with God here and now. God's grace is our greatest source of strength and love and transforming power.

God wants all of us to have grace because that is what we need to live in the kingdom here and now, not just after we die. But it isn't cheap, as Jesus' life, death and resurrection demonstrate. When you truly appreciate what a blessing it is to have been given God's grace, then that gift is not an excuse to behave badly; it is a strong motivator to behave better. As Dietrich Bonhoeffer said of Martin Luther's decision to leave the safety of the monastery to serve God in the world, once he appreciated God's gracious forgiveness, "The grace he had received was costly grace. It was grace, for it was like water on parched ground, comfort in tribulation, freedom from the bondage of a self-chosen way and forgiveness of all his sins. And it was costly, for, so far from dispensing him from good works, it meant that he must take the call to discipleship more seriously than ever before."[22] Do you think the workers in the parable who were generously blessed saw the gift as an opportunity to sleep in the next day? Unlikely. After having been treated so generously by the vineyard owner, I bet they were ready to go at sunup the next day out of gratitude alone.

All of this would be easier for us to accept of course, if Jesus had just spoken plainly and not used an economic parable to make his point. Bring money and labor into the picture, and it's hard for us to think metaphorically, let alone theologically. We get so defensive. But the economic aspect of this parable still can teach us something important

---

[22] Bonhoeffer, Dietrich, <u>Discipleship</u> (Minneapolis: Fortress Press, 2003), 49.

if we lower our hackles enough to let it. For people who are not as materially blessed as we are, who do not find it easy to earn a daily living wage, this parable speaks volumes about grace because it is a labor-based economic parable.

Liberation theologian Justo Gonzales recognized this when he read the laborers in the vineyard parable to predominately Hispanic audiences. Instead of crying out "Unfair!" when the workers were hired at the end of the day and still paid a living wage, the congregations applauded! He said, "These are people who identify with the problems of field workers. They understand the laborer who travels in his pickup truck trying to find work with little success, or even if he finds work, he is standing around waiting until the job materializes. They understand that the people looking for work need a day's pay to survive. They rejoice, then, at the grace that is not contrary to justice, but that flows with justice. They are paid what they need and deserve [as human beings] rather than the wages they might have been paid had society's concept of justice prevailed."[23] Think of all the people who have no work and desperately want it. Think of those who struggle just to have enough to feed their families each day. When we consider the story through the lens of those who find it a privilege to get to work at all, then we are the ones who seem unfairly blessed because the powers and systems of our world are stacked so heavily in our favor. Fairness is in the eye of the beholder. Isn't it better then, that God, who alone can see the big picture none of us can fully see, gets to be the one to dispense the grace?

Episcopal priest Charlotte Cleghorn once wrote that "Assumptions are planned resentments."[24] If we assume that only certain people are worthy of God's grace then that is true. We might as well plan on living life steeped with resentment over all the undeserving people who seem to get windfall blessings material or spiritual. If we assume that anything that generously benefits another necessarily devalues us, or is unfair to us, then we will spend many a day sulking with evil eyes. But what if we assume instead, that all people are beloved to God and therefore equally deserving of justice, mercy, fairness and love no matter who they are or what they do? What if we approached life in

---

[23] Gonzalez, Justo, <u>Santa Biblia: The Bible through Hispanic Eyes</u> (Nashville: Abingdon Press, 1996), 62-63.
[24] Cleghorn, Charlotte Dudley, <u>Feasting on the Word</u>, Year A, Vol. 4 (Louisville: Westminster John Knox Press, 2008), 92.

the same way that human beings approach the Ultimatum game, assuming that when it comes to sharing a generous gift, equal shares is the only fair way to go? Wouldn't that be a win-win for everyone? By the grace of God may we dare to assume so much that in our work and in our play, instead of having evil eyes and hearts filled with resentment, our hearts will be forever filled with gratitude, and our eyes with looks of love. Amen.

Transformation Triptych
Luke 9:28-43

Today is Transfiguration Sunday. Every year on the Sunday before Ash Wednesday, the Lectionary invites us to hear this bizarre, mysterious story about how Jesus went up a mountain with some of his disciples, and was transformed physically from the wise, sweat-and-blood teacher his disciples knew and loved, into a glowing godlike being for the duration of a special meeting with Moses and Elijah. The story marks a critical transition point in the direction of Jesus' ministry. Before his mountain top experience, he was still a local miracle man, a provocative and prophetic rabbi. But after his mountain top meeting, Jesus' eyes and heart were set on Jerusalem and all he knew would happen there. So, we visit this text once a year to stand where the original disciples stood, right before we too must set our own eyes and hearts on Jerusalem for Lent. In so doing we are given a memorable reminder of the divinity of Christ before we are called to walk through the valley of the shadow of death with him and out the other side.

But the story of the Transfiguration can serve as more than a literary transition or liturgical bookmark if we take some time to contemplate what happened down below the mountain as well as on top. Then the whole story becomes a thought-provoking illustration not just of the divinity of Christ, but also of the highs and lows of discipleship. The text speaks to the ways in which we experience God's presence and God's absence as we strive to journey in faith. So today, if you'll allow me to indulge my imagination a bit, I want us to do more than stand where the main characters stood; I want us to walk in their spiritual shoes for a few minutes.

The Transfiguration According to Simon Peter *(Preached from a stool behind the lectern)*

He always realized that about him, but he could never pass up a chance to make a pun on words, good or bad. Anyway, I think one of the reasons Jesus chose me to go up the mountain with him was because I recognized who he was. Just a week before the hike, he was asking the twelve of us who people were saying he was and who we thought he was; I said he was the Messiah. So, he invited me, and my buddies James and John, to go up a mountain to pray. We were like his special inner circle ever since we alone got to see him raise Jairus' daughter from the dead.

After an all-day hike to get to the top of the mountain, Jesus began praying; and I've got to admit I kind of zoned out for a while. I'm a fisherman not a mountain man, so the hike had left me kind of whipped. And he went on and on and on. But he got my full attention again when suddenly there was a blindingly bright light. Then instead of seeing Jesus, whose appearance I know as well as my own brother's, I felt like I was watching one of those glowing creatures out of that old movie "Cocoon". You know in the movie when the aliens sort of unzipped their human skin and became these creatures of light? It was kind of like that except that Jesus' skin was still on. It's hard to describe. But he glowed like an angel or God. While he was glowing there, two others arrived. Don't ask me how, but somehow I just knew they were Moses and Elijah. I was so freaked out by the whole sight of a glowing Jesus, Moses and Elijah standing only 20 feet away from me, that I didn't pay attention to what they were talking about – something about an exodus in Jerusalem. I knew that Jesus was God's chosen Messiah, but I never expected this. I could barely breathe. I didn't ask him, but I bet Moses felt the same way when he saw his burning bush.

When I finally could talk, I offered to make booths for them all because that's what we do on Succoth to celebrate the Exodus. I didn't mean anything disrespectful by the suggestion. I was just awestruck and wanted to honor them. But I guess it was the wrong thing to say because a terrifying dark cloud came over the mountain, replacing the light show, commanding me to listen to Jesus. After that I didn't know whether to feel elated or ashamed. The whole experience seemed timeless, yet it hardly lasted any time at all. When we went back down and joined the others, I didn't tell them what I saw. I figure if Jesus wanted them to know about it he would have invited them or told them. And I didn't need them telling me that I was nuts, or just dreaming, or that I messed up with my booth remark. Still, between you and me, it was amazing in the beginning, when all the light was there. It felt like being in heaven, like being right next to God. I wish I could feel like that all the time. If I had understood what would happen to Jesus only a short time after we came back down, if I had understood about the cross, I don't think I would have come down. But now we have been through and seen so much darkness that the whole thing is starting to feel like it was just a dream.

The Transfiguration According to Andrew (*preached from the foot of the chancel*)

Before I say anything else, let me just remind you that I was the one who started following Jesus first. People always forget that about me. They all know my brother Simon because he was the charismatic, passionate and impulsive one. I was more of the strong silent type. But I was the one who introduced Simon to Jesus. Like everyone else, Jesus seemed to take to Simon more than to me. So, he's the one who got to go with Jesus on a private mountain top prayer retreat, not me. When they left, along with those thunderheads, James and John, I don't mind telling you that I was more than a little bit irritated being stuck at the bottom of the mountain, waiting with the rest of the group.

We thought we would just hang out and relax for a while, but it wasn't long after Jesus left that all hell broke loose, literally. A man came to us with a demon-possessed son and wanted us to heal him. As if we have that kind of power! The demon tortured the boy, making him shake all over and even almost roll into the fire once. We did our best but we couldn't heal him. I've never felt so alone, so helpless; I've never wanted God so much. We prayed and prayed and prayed so hard. Then Jesus returned with the others. Simon had a kind of weird expression on his face, but I didn't have time to ask him what his deal was because the demon began going at the boy. Jesus seemed tired, and sad, and kind of cranky from his hike. But you know what? He healed that boy on the spot. And in that moment, even though it was just Jesus, it was like I was standing in the presence of God. I felt the same way when Jesus calmed the storm which almost killed us when we were at sea, and when he healed that old woman who had been bleeding. It's hard to describe. I knew then he was no ordinary guy. And I knew I wasn't alone any more.

I don't know if Simon Peter or Andrew and the other disciples who were left down below ever had these thoughts of course. But I like the way that today's text juxtaposes a mountain top experience with a valley-of-the-shadow-of-death experience of God because both experiences can teach us about the presence of God. A lot of people dream of having a mountain top experience, and are jealous of those who have experienced something otherworldly or supernatural. But not everyone has these experiences. Moreover, as today's text reveals indirectly, burning bush or mountain top experiences are a mixed blessing. In the moment, they are incredibly powerful. But after they are done, then what? Peter was in Jesus' inner circle. He saw Jesus perform unbelievably powerful miracles, recognized that Jesus was the Messiah, and even got to see him illuminated like God. Yet the memory of those events did not prevent him from betraying Jesus in the courtyard of the high priest Caiaphas. Did he forget that Jesus was

God then? I don't know. But I do know that it can be hard to hold onto the brilliant intimacy of a mountain top experience day in and day out, in a challenging world. Once you have heard the voice of God, or experienced in such a powerful way the presence of God, it doesn't stop you from yearning for another experience; and in the meantime, not hearing God's voice any more can make it feel as though the God you knew intimately has abandoned you.

Author Christian Wiman writes about this in his book, My Bright Abyss.[25] As a child he had an encounter with God in church which was so powerful and transforming that it made him flee the sanctuary. He was found curled up weeping and mumbling in ecstatic awe hidden in the church basement. But by the time he was an adult, the people he met would have assumed he was an atheist. He didn't talk about his experience for fear people would think he was crazy; and after a while the whole experience seemed like a distant dream to him that was easy to rationalize away when he was confronted with the very real challenges of his life. Looking back, he writes, "I can't tell which is worse, standing numb and apart from the world, wanting Being to burn me awake, or feeling that fire too acutely to crave anything other than escape into everydayness. What I do know is that the turn toward God has not lessened my anxieties, and I find myself continually falling back into wounds, wishes, terrors I thought I had risen above."[26]

Then there are those who, like Andrew in my imagination, never get to see a burning bush or a glow-in-the-dark Jesus, who discover that God feels most real just when it seems like all-hell is breaking loose. For those people, it is almost as though the Transfiguration is reversed. I have been blessed to know multiple people like this, who, while they were dying of cancer, positively glowed from being in the presence of God. They didn't get a miracle, but they felt God in the love of family and the generosity of friends and the support of the community so acutely that you would think they had been transfigured by some kind of mountain top experience. Until they died, they testified with joy that God can be found even in the valley

---

[25] Wiman, Christian, My Bright Abyss: Meditations of a Modern Believer (New York: Farrar, Straus and Giroux, 2013).
[26] *Ibid*, 9.

of the shadow of death, and that suffering does not mean divine abandonment.

Rev. Spencer Morgan Rice, who was Rector of Trinity Church in Boston once told of an experience he had early in his ministry when he was serving a small congregation in L.A., which brought this lesson home for him:

Every day a man would come in at 12:15 p.m., walk down the center aisle, stare at the cross in the chancel, and then leave. Rice worried about him because the man looked homeless. He was unwashed and shabbily dressed and unsteady on his feet. But when they offered him help, he said, "No thank you. I just come in every day and stand before the cross and say, 'Jesus, it's Jim.' It's not much of a prayer, I know, but I think God knows what I mean."

Well months went by and the man stopped coming. One morning Rice got a call from the mother superior of a home for aged men run by the Sisters of the Transfiguration, of all things. She told him that Jim had been admitted. When Rice came to visit him, she said, 'You know, when Jim first came here he went into the most cantankerous ward we have. Everyone here has tried without success to bring some joy and calm to that ward, and failed. Jim went in and transformed the place. So, I went and asked him two days ago how he was able to bring so much joy and peace to the men. He said, 'Oh Sister, it's because of my visitor.' I know he has not had a single visitor for the last two months. So, I said, 'Jim, what visitor? I've never seen a visitor.' And he said, 'Sister, every day at 12:00 he comes and stands at the foot of my bed and says, "Jim, it's Jesus."'"[27]

I don't know if this is a true story or not. But I know that God says, "Jim," or "Sandy" or "Mike," or "Mary, it's Jesus," in both extraordinary and ordinary ways. We need only to open our eyes and ears. So, there is no need for us to be jealous of one another, to battle about who is the greatest, as all the disciples did twice after the Transfiguration. There is no need to worry that God has abandoned us either, whether we have always been at the bottom, or were once blessed to go to the top. No one, not even the human Jesus, gets to

---

[27] Edited Illustration listed under "transfiguration" in *Animating Illustrations Library*, HOMILETICSONLINE (http://www.homilecticsonline.com/subscriber/illustration_search.asp?keywords' transfiguration). (Used with permission.)

stay forever on the mountain top in this life. What then, do you think we might we learn about our walk of discipleship from walking in Jesus' human shoes in this story?

The Transfiguration According to Jesus *(Preached from behind the communion table)*

I was so eager to get to the top that I almost dragged Peter and James and John up the last stretch of the way. My ministry was picking up momentum and opponents with equal speed. I yearned to reconnect so badly, already afraid I wouldn't have the courage to do what I knew I was called to do. "Abba" I prayed when we got to the top. "Abba, I want to be with you. Abba, give me strength for the hard road ahead." Then God and I were one again in a way I hadn't felt since my baptism. Oh to feel the confidence and comfort of that union again! It was so wonderful. Then God sent me old friends to build up my confidence still more: Moses, who knew what it was like to try to lead a stubborn and lost people; and Elijah, who dared to do what I sometimes dream of doing, running from the darkness to hide in a cave when he was overwhelmed. I joked with Moses about how easy he had had it. All he had to do was write God's word on stone; I must write it on stubborn and closed-off human hearts![28] Then almost on cue, Peter broke the spell. Oh, my dear friend, ever a bull in a china shop. If you only knew what lay ahead for you, that there would be a cross with your name on it, too, one day, then maybe you would have been quicker to listen to my holy encouragers instead of trying to reel in the moment like a great catch. But you didn't know. You couldn't. So, I became the human Son again, and listened to my Father's voice outside myself, defensive on my behalf.

At the foot of the mountain the others were completely lost. After the joy of being one with God, being sent back to a place of so much doubt and need felt like a cruel punishment at first. I, too, found myself wishing we could have stayed on the mountain top. "Don't leave me here in the trenches, Abba!" Then I saw the joy and relief in Andrew's eyes at my return, and knew I was where I needed to be. How can I look at their fear and not answer? How can I look at a young boy's pain and not be moved? It is for them, these often bumbling and blind people that I have come. It is for the seeking and the sinful that I will go to

---

[28] This line was inspired by U.A. Fanthorpe's poem, *"Getting It Across"*, as quoted in Loder, Ted, <u>The Haunt of Grace: Responses to the Mystery of God's Presence </u>(Philadelphia: Innisfree Press, Inc., 2002), 35.

Elizabeth Dallas McLean

Jerusalem. There is no place to run and no need to hide. I know that Abba will be ever with me as I am with them. Together we will set them free! Amen.

Sin No More Ash Wednesday
Psalm 51:1-5; John 7:53- 8:11

"Let anyone among you who is without sin be the first to throw a stone at her," Jesus said when confronted by an angry crowd which wanted to stone to death a woman charged with adultery. Twelve years ago, when I first saw Brad Sherrill, the actor who was here last month with his show APOSTLE, perform this scene in his first show, *The Gospel of John*. I was taken aback when he, in character as Jesus, walked up to me and offered me a stone. He wasn't singling me out; he tried to give it to many others in the audience that day as well. But everyone had the same reaction that I did. "Get that thing away from me!" In that very convicting moment, none of us wanted to judge another or to be judgmental. We knew that we could not possibly claim to be without sin, and therefore were in no position to condemn the sin of another. As *John* records, the elders in the crowd in Jesus' day knew this too; so, they were the first to lay down their stones and slink away.

But were that scene to play out today, particularly outside the context of a Church, I wonder if the result would be the same? Our culture has such an odd approach to sin these days. On the one hand, the problems of our world have now been so psychologized and politicized that I suspect more people would be repulsed now by the suggestion that they *are* sinners than that they are not. We live in an age of "I'm OK, you're OK," when parents are told to focus only on the positive with their children because pointing out the negative could damage their self-esteem. We live in an age when lawyers argue with straight faces that their clients must not be held responsible for their crimes because they ate too many Twinkies or were raised in such affluence that they cannot be expected to know right from wrong. Now we have excuses for everything we do, and speak of our faults and our hurtful actions in terms of brokenness, weakness, or insensitivity, not sin, and confess in the ever-popular passive voice: "Mistakes were made."

On the other hand, we have not abandoned the idea that other people are terrible sinners worthy of our condemnation. Our culture loves condemning others for anything and everything. Sins of lust still get a lot of attention. But society is also happy to judge and condemn others for weight gain, weight loss, liberal politics, conservative politics, sexual orientation, marital status, ideology and a whole host of other behaviors. Social media and smart phones have made it easy for people to threaten others with career-destroying, relationship-destroying, life-destroying verbal stones; and even self-professed Christians, like Jerry Falwell's son, the President of Liberty University, encourage those who will listen, to go ahead and throw stones at certain people, or better yet, ditch the stones in favor of a more powerful and efficient means of imposing lethal punishment-- the kind that comes with ammunition.[29]

These trends reveal that humanity has not stopped sinning, not by a long shot. But we have forgotten what the Bible teaches about sin and humanity's relationship with it. The point of the concept is not to empower us to condemn others, nor is it to shred our self-esteem. The point of the concept is to remind us that there are moral and spiritual dimensions to life in addition to psychological and physical ones, dimensions which equip us to identify right from wrong with God's help, and which affect the community as well as the individual. The point of using the word "sin" is to name humanity's problem, not to excuse it, so that we will recognize both our responsibility for the world's brokenness and our need for God to heal it.

Author and columnist David Brooks put it this way. He said the word "sin" reminds us that "the most essential parts of life are matters of individual responsibility and moral choice: whether to be brave or cowardly, honest or deceitful, compassionate or callous, faithful or loyal." When we use other words because we don't like the word "sin," "that doesn't make life any less moral.... It just means we think and talk about these choices less clearly, and thus become increasingly blind to the moral stakes of everyday life.... If you take away the concept of sin, then you take away the thing the good

---

[29] See e.g. Botelho, Greg, "*Liberty University president encourages students to be armed*", CNN.COM, (posted 9:43 PM ET, Sat Dec. 5, 2015), retrieved Feb. 7, 2016 from http://www.cnn.com/2015/12/05/us/liberty-university-urges-armed-students.

person struggles against", the thing that builds character and integrity and human goodness.[30]

Perhaps even more importantly for the sake of our world, if you take away the concept of sin, you also take away our clear connectedness to our neighbor. Errors may be made by individuals and fixed by individuals. But sin always has a communal nature. That is bad in terms of the possibility for harm. But it is good in the sense that becoming aware of one's own sinfulness tends to make one more sympathetic toward others who sin, not less. As the Apostle Paul said to the Christians in Rome, "We have all sinned and fallen short of the glory of God." (Rom. 3:23). In other words, when you confess to your own sinfulness, not just your weakness or insensitivity, it becomes much harder to pick up and throw stones.

As Christians, we confess our sins regularly before God and one another in worship. But recognizing that sin is communal as well as individual, once a year we also put on the ashes of penitence on our foreheads for all to see. We do not do this to so that we will be justified walking around the Giant later with feelings of moral superiority, or so that we can punish ourselves with public shaming. We do this because in addition to wanting to name publicly that sin is at the heart of humanity's problems, we also want to name publicly the solution. Humanity needs the redeeming grace of God.

Think of it this way: If our problems were purely psychological, we could solve them with therapy. If they were purely environmental, we could solve them by changing our environment. But they are not. The root of our problem is moral and spiritual, and for that we need God. Until our culture admits this, the problems will continue. But the good news of the Gospel which our foreheads will also proclaim tonight is that we do not need to be afraid or ashamed to admit this because while we were still sinners, Christ died for us. He did not come to condemn us, but to enable us to have abundant life. So, if we turn to him, with the help of the Spirit, we all can sin less; we can learn to make better choices.

---

[30] Brooks, David, The Road to Character (New York: Random House, 2015), 54 55.

Lent is a season for us to embrace the two truths the ashes will proclaim: that we are all sinners, and that our redemption comes from God, not our own cleverness or willpower. Lent is a time for us to strive to turn, or return to God with humility and honesty, so that God can help us with our daily struggle to make the right choices for ourselves and our world. But you don't have to wear ashes for 40 days to help you do this. Tonight, in addition to marking you as both a vulnerable sinner and a beloved recipient of the saving grace of God, I will also be inviting you to take with you a small stone. Put it in your pocket, or on your desk, or in your car and give it a squeeze every time you find yourselves thinking how awful someone else is and how much better you are. Pick it up also on days when you are feeling guilty about your own sinfulness, as a reminder that what awaits us at the end of the season is not condemnation, but a tomb with the stone rolled away.

"I do not understand my own actions. For I do not do what I want, but I do the very thing I hate.... I can will what is right, but I cannot do it," Paul bemoaned (Rom. 7:15). We've all been there, so there is no need for us to try to deny it to ourselves or to others. The solution to our problem is not to stop using the word sin, but like the woman whose life Jesus spared, to try to go and sin no more ourselves. No one can do this perfectly. But it is good to have something to battle against instead of each other. And when we confess our sins, through the grace of God in Jesus Christ, we connect with the one who has the power to help us sin less. That is good news both for our sakes and for the sake of our world. Amen.

What Do You See?

Job 19:25-27a; John 20:1-18

About eight years ago, a British firm called "Transport for London" made a short commercial as a part of a public safety campaign for cyclists. Called *"The Awareness Test,"* the commercial invited viewers to test their awareness by watching some young people play basketball. The commercial was such a huge hit in England that soon Facebook users all over the globe, who are known for their love of self-assessment quizzes of all kinds, were happily taking the test and sharing their own results. Maybe you remember doing that? In any case, since the *Gospel of John* says that Mary Magdalene mistook the risen Christ for the gardener, I thought that it might be helpful before we consider why she did, and what that must do with our celebrating Easter today, for all of us to use the brief test to check out own vision. In case you have trouble hearing or understanding the instructions, let me just tell you that the quiz instructions are to count the total number of times that the basketball players wearing white pass the ball to each other. If you already know the answer, don't tell your neighbor until it's over. OK let's watch.[31] *[The video clip, "Do the Test" from YouTube was shown. In it the basketball players pass the ball 13 times. Also, in the middle of the action, a man in a bear costume does the moonwalk.]*

Did you see it? Did you see the moonwalking bear? Maybe you are a highly observant person, able to count and watch at the same time and did see it. But I am not, and certainly did not see the bear the first time I saw this video; I was too intent on focusing on the players in white. Most people I know who have taken the test miss the bear for the same reason. But if the point of the commercial is to remind us that bicycles on the road are hard to see if we aren't actively looking for them, then think how much harder it was for the first disciples to see the risen Christ! We need some new term which is even stronger than "unexpected" to convey just how much the disciples were not looking for Jesus that morning in the garden. Even though he had told them repeatedly that "the Son of Man would rise again

---

[31] Transport for London, (Mar. 11, 2008). *Test Your Awareness: Do the Test* [Video] Retrieved Mar. 21, 2016, from http://www.youtube.com/watch?v'e5zGeHAv9VA.

in three days," his pronouncement was so cryptic and outside of their understanding about God and the laws of the universe, that the disciples were still completely blindsided by both the empty tomb and the even more miraculous Resurrection. Barely three days after they had watched in horror as the one they thought was the Messiah was crucified and buried, they had only just begun to grasp the unexpected and grim reality that Jesus was dead. So, when they went to the garden that morning, they were not actively looking for the "Lord of the Dance" to cross their path. As we were when we took the awareness test, they were too busy focusing on other things.

Mary Magdalene was consumed with loss when she showed up in the garden that morning. In the *Gospel of John*, she doesn't come with spices to anoint the body, which she knew was sealed behind a rock too big to move. She doesn't come with other women either. She comes alone in the dark before dawn because she is not ready to let go of Jesus. She needed to be near him, to stand on one side of the tomb knowing he was on the other. So, when she saw the tomb was open and empty, her first reaction wasn't joy, it was panic. Someone had clearly stolen the body; what other explanation could there be? The thought so consumed her that even after Peter and the one disciple, possibly John, had come and gone, she could not see anything other than the absence of her Lord. When the two angels showed up in the tomb, she did not fall on the ground in awe and fear as people usually do when they encounter angels in the Bible; she treated them more like hospital orderlies who had changed her loved one's room while she went for a cup of coffee in the cafeteria. "Where have you moved the body?" she demanded. She was so focused on the loss of Jesus that she could not even see him when he was standing in front of her face.

If you have ever lost a spouse or other close loved one, then you probably can understand Mary's heart-broken fog. In the early stages of grief, it is not uncommon to feel like you are traveling in a state of suspended animation or trance. You lose track of time, of objects, of conversations. When did you last eat? Who knows? Did you remember to call Aunt Bette? "Yes. No... Wait what?" Add to that fog the fact that Resurrection was inconceivable, and Mary's mistaking Jesus for the gardener makes perfect sense.

Peter and John are not any more aware than Mary in *John's* account. They are not blinded by the same kind of fog of grief, however; they seem focused more on themselves than on Jesus. First they reject the fact that Mary could have been telling them the truth about the tomb. They must go check it out themselves. Then they race to the tomb like overgrown children more concerned with who is the fastest than what they will find. "I beat you to the tomb!" "Well I went in before you did!" Could their self-absorption have had to do with their own grief? Perhaps. Maybe they, like Mary, could not yet let go of Jesus and were unconsciously still trying to prove their devotion to him. But I still imagine that if they had stuck around in the garden with Mary instead of leaving, the risen Christ might have greeted them with the gentle chastisement: "Don't tell me you are *still* fighting over who is the greatest, boys?"

They did not stick around to see him, however. Once they confirmed that Mary was telling the truth, they left the garden to go back to where the rest of the disciples were hiding. They did not go looking for the body or searching for muddy incriminating foot prints in the garden first. They did not risk bringing attention to themselves by consulting the authorities for help on the way home. They did not even pause to ask each other why grave robbers would have unbound Jesus from his burial wrappings before taking his body. The evidence that something unexpected and extraordinary was in front of their faces, but *John* makes it very clear that they did not yet understand or see the truth.

So, what can we learn from all three disciples' lack of awareness? At the very least, we can take some comfort from their experience. If the people who knew Jesus best were slow to recognize that the miraculous had happened even though Jesus told them it would, and even though he gave them front row seats for the action, then we can hardly be blamed if we have doubts now and then about the reality of the Resurrection ourselves. Two thousand years later, we cannot see how huge the boulder was that was rolled aside. We cannot see the grave clothes lying there. We cannot see angels in dazzling white or hear a gardener who looks oddly familiar calling us by name. Is it any wonder then that the whole story can seem hard to believe at times?

No. It is quite a common thing, even for faithful Christians to carry unspoken doubts about the Easter good news. But if all we take away from this story is the thought that we need not feel ashamed if we doubt, then we have missed the more important lesson in *John's* Easter account. He wrote his gospel for readers who lived long after the Resurrection. The first people to read his gospel could not see the stone or the linens any more than we can. So, he told his version of events in such a way to make it clear that it doesn't matter whether we have seen those things. Even if we had been given the chance to see them, we probably would not have understood their significance any more than Mary, Peter and "the disciple whom Jesus loved" did if we, like they, were not looking for the risen Christ. In other words, *John's* account of Jesus' Resurrection is the gospel equivalent of the awareness test for us, only this time we know the punch line. We know that they missed the bear. That means we don't have to miss him ourselves. We can learn from the first disciples a powerful lesson about faith and human blindness, and about the importance of actively looking for the signs of God's promises that are right in front of our faces.

W. P. Lemon once said, "Easter is not a passport to another world; it is a quality of perception for this one." [32] The good news that we are celebrating today is that God's love is more powerful than human sin. Human hatred could not defeat it; human violence couldn't kill it. The good news we are celebrating today is that God has the power and the desire to give us and our world new life, and will stop at nothing to get the message through to us. The good news we are celebrating today is that nothing on earth or in heaven can ever separate us from the love of God in Christ Jesus, and therefore we need not fear. Yes, Easter reveals to us a life beyond this life that God wants us to have; the message of heaven is part of the good news today. But most of the good news is about here and now, about how much we are loved, and how much better our world can be. That means that Easter is not simply something that will become real to us only when we die. It is real now, if only we have eyes to perceive it.

Mary could not see because she was consumed with loss. Her sorrow, her sadness, her fear acted like blinders. The same is true for us. We can miss the good news of God's presence, and miss the opportunities for new life God gives us in Christ, if all we focus on is the bad news that drives the headlines. We can miss experiencing God's saving love if all we do is focus on how much our lives are not the way we wanted them to be, or count how many ways we have been hurt, or how many reasons we should be afraid.

---

[32] As quoted in THE LIVING PULPIT, Jan.- Mar. 1998, Vol. 7, No. 1, 31.

We can also miss out on the good news of Easter if all we focus on is ourselves like Peter and John. This is true whether we are focusing on ourselves in a positive or negative way. When we are determined to prove that we are the greatest, then it is easy to forget that salvation is not a prize we can win or lose. We can make our entire lives one big stressful competition, or turn ourselves into idols, instead of being liberated by the knowledge that we do not have to work to be the best to earn God's love and grace. Likewise, if we focus on ourselves in a negative way, constantly looking for the evidence which confirms our belief that we are not good enough or worthy of love, we can end up spending our whole lives miserable, never seeing the God who loves us so much he gave his life for us. The good news of Easter is that we all are saved by God's mercy, and all are blessed by God's grace. There is no need to prove that we are the best, nor any need to condemn ourselves for being the worst.

The late, great Christian folk singer David Bailey once captured the essence of John's Easter message in a funny little song he wrote called *"Takes Two to See."* It wasn't intended to be an Easter message, but it is nonetheless. The first verse goes:

Sherlock and Watson went camping;
Sherlock said, "What do you see?"
Watson said, "I see the North Star
shining over me.
Over there I see the Big Dipper,
tucked behind Orion's belt."
Sherlock said, "Watson, you moron-
someone has stolen our tent."
Watson said, "Sherlock, you're right,
but look beyond your discovery.
You saw what was missing right before your eyes,
but you missed an entire galaxy."[33]

Today we celebrate the most extraordinary, world-changing, inconceivable truth that God has seen the worst that humanity can do and decided to love us forever anyway. Instead of smiting us for our sins, or leaving us to wallow in our own pride and shame-filled ways, God has

---

[33] David M. Bailey, *"Takes Two to See,"* TAKES TWO TO SEE, 2006. Retrieved from http://www.cdbaby.com/cd/dmbailey06. ©2006 David M. Bailey (used with permission.) See also Davidmbailey.com and https://www.facebook.com/David-M-Bailey-176097525734660

chosen to do the most dramatic thing imaginable, to come back from the dead, so that we will finally open our eyes. On that first Easter morning, the risen Christ began to birth a new creation for all of us. Even now God is showering us with redeeming grace and leading us into healing newness. But the risen Christ and his new creation are visible only if we only have eyes to see.

Are you missing galaxies because you are focused on a stolen tent? Are you missing the risen Christ because you expect to see only gardeners? We have heard from those who were there that the stone was rolled away. The linen wrappings were left behind. There were angels in white waiting with good news in the tomb. Hold that evidence in your heart and then strive to look at the world in a different way. If you want to see the risen Christ, you will see the Lord dancing wherever people are helping or loving each other instead of ignoring or hating each other. You will see him wherever people are showing mercy instead of judging others. You may even hear him call your name, in moments when you are given the chance to think about or see yourself or someone else in a whole new way, in moments when you are invited to venture into new territory, or to leave old hurts behind.

God is with us! Shout alleluia! Christ isn't dead; he is raised! And that means we can be raised too, in this life and the next. Instead of nursing your pain and your fears, instead of relentlessly counting your accomplishments or your failures, look for Christ in the garden and beyond. He is here and even now calling all who have eyes to see to follow him into hope, peace, joy and abundant new life. Thanks be to God! Amen

The Eternal Now
Ecclesiastes 3:1-8; Matthew 6:25-34

"For everything there is a season, and a time for every matter under heaven," the author of *Ecclesiastes*, known as "the Preacher," famously wrote. People often choose these words for funerals because they give us some small measure of comfort in their reminder that there is a time for everything, even for death. But in Alan Lightman's thought-provoking little book Einstein's Dreams,[34] these words take on a whole new meaning when the main character dreams, not of a time for everything, but of every kind of time. In each chapter, Lightman describes a world in which time itself is understood in a unique way, different from our own. For example, in one world, people live their whole lives in a single day, so time is understood both as precious and fleeting.[35] No one forms lasting relationships in this world, or even has much time for conversation; everyone is busy trying to cram in everything life should have in 24 hours. In another world, time is a sixth sense, perceived differently by different people, in much the same way that taste and sound are perceived differently in ours.[36] Some people feel that time is flying by, while others feel it dragging painfully. In still another, time is a visible dimension, a road that each person can see leading off into the distant future.[37] You can choose how quickly you want to travel the road, but you cannot go backwards once you're on it. So some people choose to stop at a favorite moment and cherish it forever, rather than leave it behind. Others are so eager to get to a certain stage of their lives that they race on ahead, only to discover, too late, after they reach their temporal destination, that while they sprinted ahead, huge chunks of their lives passed by in a blur never to be recovered.

I have read the book several times, and never get tired of thinking about what it would be like if time were for us as it is for people in Einstein's Dreams. For example, would you build your house on stilts on a mountain top, if you knew that time moved more slowly

---

[34] Lightman, Alan, Einstein's Dreams (New York: Pantheon Books, 1993).
[35] *Ibid*, 107-11.
[36] *Ibid*, 112-16.
[37] *Ibid*, 133-37.

at higher elevations? Would you spend all your time trying to capture time, if it was like a flighty bird? The book is fiction but Lightman's observation that the way we understand and respond to time affects everything in our lives, is still clear and true. We've all known people who waste time while others chase it. We've seen how some people are willing to spend crazy amounts of money trying to erase the effects of time on their bodies, while others strive to grow up far too quickly and shortchange their lives in the process.

Most people I know feel that there never seems to be enough time to get everything done, to try all the things that would be interesting to try, and to learn all the things that would be interesting to learn. In our Western culture, which is far-more time-oriented than some others, a lot of people spend much of their lives with the same frantic expression on their faces that Lucille Ball had in the famous *I Love Lucy* episode in which she must work in a chocolate factory. Unable to keep up with the chocolates passing her by on the conveyor belt, Lucy starts madly grabbing at them and stuffing them in her shirt and her mouth and anyplace else she can find to stop their relentless forward advance.

In the Bible, time neither makes people as frantic as it does today, nor does it come in as many forms as it does in Einstein's Dreams. There are only three different understandings woven together throughout the Old and New Testaments. But how we allow these times to shape us makes all the difference in our discipleship. The first kind of time is basic calendar and clock time, known in Greek as *chronos*. This time marks the hours and days, the seasons and appointed holidays. The second kind of time is eternity, a time outside of all time, in which God, the Alpha and Omega, the beginning and end, abides, and in which, through Christ, we all will dwell someday. Peter tries to describe this kind of time when he reminded his readers that "with the Lord, one day is like a thousand years, and a thousand years are like one day." (2 Pet. 3:8).

But it is the third kind of biblical time, called *kairos* in the Greek, that I want us to think about today because it is this kind of time which today's Scripture lessons address. In the Greek Old Testament known as the Septuagint, *Ecclesiastes* reads, "For everything there is a season (*chronos*), and a *kairos* for everything under heaven." The list of activities seems to suggest clock time. But *kairos* is not clock time; and although it is God's time, it is not eternity outside of time either. *Kairos* is what theologian Paul Tillich called "the eternal now," a kind of time within our time when God's grace "breaks powerfully into our consciousness and gives us the certainty of the eternal, or a dimension of time which cuts into time and gives us our time."[38]

Tillich was fond of dense philosophical definitions like this one, which make you scratch your head and think, "Wait... what?" But you don't have to be a German theologian to understand or experience *kairos*. If you have ever been blessed to spend time with children, you've probably experienced it. Mothers often experience it when they get to hold their babies for the first time, and the whole world seems to fall away leaving only the two of you to gaze at each other. You don't need to call the child your own to experience this however. The odds are good that if you spend time with any children you will get at least a little sense of *kairos* through them because children are born living in *kairos*. They naturally live in the present moment, since they do not have the memories to enable them to live in the past, nor the responsibilities to make them worry about the future. They notice every little bug and stone on walks, oblivious to how long they are taking. They become so easily lost in play that they do not understand why parents get so antsy about schedules and bed times. Life is all about whatever is happening right now, so much so that it takes years of adults cajoling and nagging to shift their sense of time enough to make them dwell in *chronos* instead.

Adults can still experience *kairos*, however, even without the help of a child. Some people do when they fall in love, and suddenly discover that time stands still when they gaze into the eyes of their beloved, or that talking with them can make hours seem like minutes. Others experience *kairos* when someone they love is dying. When *chronos* is running out, *kairos* kicks in again making every present moment with the person feel sacred it is so steeped in love and gratitude and outreach to God. Some people also experience *kairos* when doing something creative - playing music or painting, while others find *kairos* communing with nature, or reaching out to God in prayer or meditation. *Kairos* is any time when we can experience the sacred

---

[38] Tillich, Paul, The Eternal Now (New York: Charles Scribner's Sons, 1963), 131.

eternal in the now, when we are able, for a few seconds or hours or days to live in a state of acute appreciation of the blessings of the present, instead of a state of preoccupation with what has happened in the past, or what lies ahead in the future.

In her book, Stroke of Insight, Dr. Jill Bolte Taylor writes about how she discovered the wonders of *kairos* after suffering a massive stroke.[39] Taylor was only in her mid-thirties when a blood vessel in her temporal lobe ruptured, sending blood throughout her whole left brain, rendering it largely useless. She lost her ability to speak, read or understand words, as well as her understanding of numbers. She also lost access to her memories and her dreams because the part of her brain that organized life in a linear fashion into past, present and future was taken off-line. All that was left to her initially was her right brain, which is hardwired to live every moment in the now. It sounds like everyone's worst nightmare. But Taylor did not feel fear, grief or anger in that moment; to her surprise, she felt a rarely experienced kind of peace and oneness with God. Like an adult suddenly given a toddler brain, she was kicked back into *kairos*, and noticed again all the little things that make life filled with wonder and joy. And like a toddler, she resented her therapists when they wanted her to relearn how to live by *chronos* again. She didn't want to reclaim all the worries and stresses which come from living in linear time and allowing *chronos* to be your master.

Although Taylor regained full use of her left brain after 8 years of therapy, she chose intentionally not to allow her life pattern to become enslaved again to the haunts of the past and the worries of the future. She chose, in other words, to try to remain as much as possible living in the eternal now. For those of us who are not brain damaged, but have been brainwashed by our culture to worship *chronos* (and I speak as one of them, believe me), it takes far more work to live in the eternal now than in the temporal past and future. It can be almost a spiritual battle to do so. Recognizing this, C.S. Lewis attributed the *chronos*-driven aspect of our culture to the work

---

[39] Taylor, Jill Bolte, My Stroke of Insight: A Brain Scientist's Personal Journey (New York: Plume Pub., 2006).

of demons and devils in his classic work of theological fiction called
The Screwtape Letters.[40]

In the book, a demon called Screwtape, offers these words of advice to his nephew Wormwood, about how to lead people away from God, whom he calls "the Enemy," by seducing them away from the eternal now: "The humans live in time, but our Enemy destines them to eternity. He therefore... wants them to attend chiefly to two things, to eternity itself, and to that point of time which they call the Present. For the Present is the point at which time touches eternity. Of the present moment, and of it only, humans have an experience analogous to the experience which our Enemy has of reality; in it alone freedom and actuality are offered them.... Our business is to get them away from the eternal and from the Present. With this view, we sometimes tempt a human... to live in the Past... [But] it is far better to make them live in the Future.... The future is, of all things, the thing least like eternity. ... [N]early all vices are rooted in the future. Gratitude looks to the past and love to the present; fear, avarice, lust, and ambition look ahead."[41]

Whether or not you believe in demons, Screwtape makes a powerful point, the same one that Jesus tried to make in a different way in today's gospel lesson. When we orient all our lives toward the future, even if that future is simply the soccer practice which our child must attend later in the same day, or the conference call tomorrow for which we still need to prepare, we can miss out on much of our lives, and miss out on the experience of God in the now. Worrying obsessively about tomorrow can lead us to miss the beauty of God's creation, to miss the magic moments of connection, and to miss the feelings of love and peace that come from sitting with God in the eternal now. Thus, a classic Jewish penitential prayer includes these haunting words: "Days pass, years vanish, and we walk sightless among miracles."[42] It reminds us that we can be so focused on appeasing the relentless taskmaster which is *chronos* that we rush ahead

---

[40] Lewis, C.S., The Screwtape Letters (New York: HarperCollins Pub. 1942).

[41] *Ibid*, The Screwtape Letters, 75-77, (1996 reprint edition).

[42] As quoted in L'Engle, Madeleine, Walking on Water: Reflections on Faith and Art (New York: North Point Press, 1980), 98-99.

in our lives until we cannot rush anymore, only to discover that we have not savored most of the blessings God gave us along the way.

In Thornton Wilder's classic play, *Our Town*, one of the main characters, Emily, dies in childbirth. Sitting with the other dead in the cemetery, she asks the Stage Manager if she can return home to relive just one day. Reluctantly he allows her to do so. When she does, she is overwhelmed by all that is beautiful and holy in a single ordinary day. "Mama" she cries, although her mother cannot hear her. "Mama, just look at me one minute as though you really saw me... it goes so fast we don't have time to look at one another." When she goes back to the graveyard because it is too painful to watch everyone missing so much, she asks the Stage Manager, "Do any human beings ever realize life while they live it?" He sighs and says, "No. The saints and poets maybe. They do some."[43]

The saints --isn't that who we are called to be? Those who trust so strongly in the power of God's saving grace as evidenced in humanity's past, and above all through Jesus Christ, that we do not need to worry about our futures, and instead can dwell with the eternal in the here and now? We can be responsible human beings without worshiping *chronos*. Although we may not know what the future holds, we do know who holds the future, so we are free to embrace the eternal in the now. Or to put it another way, faith can put us in the same place that Taylor found herself in, without our having to experience a massive stroke. It can put us in the position to recognize that we are closest to God in the now, and therefore enable us to make sure we do not allow *chronos* to rob us of those sacred moments as they come along. Faith can enable us to trust that the eternal is all around us, and to choose more intentionally and often to dwell in it.

When the Preacher first wrote *Ecclesiastes* in the Hebrew, and made his list of all the times of our lives, the word for time he used throughout was the Hebrew equivalent of *chronos,* calendar time. "There is a time for this and a time for that," he wrote because he was

---

[43] See *World Union Shabbat Evening Service* (World Union for Progressive Judaism, 2007), 15 (available at
http://www.wupj.org/Assets/Brochures/ShabbatService.pd)

a cynical person writing during a cynical time. He didn't seem to know about the eternal in the now, or if he did, he clearly hadn't experienced it. Not surprisingly, thus, most of *Ecclesiastes* expresses a depressing sort of resigned cynicism. "Life keeps plodding on so you might as well eat, drink and be merry because death awaits you in the future. It's all just vanity in the end." But centuries later, when Jewish leaders were deciding which texts would be Holy Scriptures, and translating them into Greek because most Jews couldn't read Hebrew any more, they changed almost all the *chronos* time references in the Preacher's famous litany into *kairos* times. In so doing, they "sanctified" time, or made it holy, which is what Rabbi Abraham Heschel said is one of the things Judaism is all about.[44]

The same is true of Christianity. Instead of worshiping time, we worship God in every present moment of our lives. We can find God in moments of life and of death. We can find God in moments of planting and plucking up what is planted. We can find God in tears and laughter, in silence and in speech. How many clocks and calendars do you have? How often do you consult them? Trust and believe the good news of the Gospel: God was with us in the past and will be with us in the future. Thus if we are looking for the right time to experience God and the eternal, no matter what time it may be, that time is now. Thanks be to God. Amen.

---

[44] Heschel, Abraham Joseph, The Sabbath (New York: Farrar, Strauss & Giroux, 1951), 10.

No Cape Required, No Parade Promised
Exodus 1:8-10; 15-21; Luke 10:1-11, 17-20

During World War II, an eight-year old girl named Francine Christophe was taken with her mother by the Nazis to the Bergen-Belsen concentration camp. Among the few items that her mother could grab before being taken away were two small pieces of chocolate. She told her daughter that she would save them for the day when they felt they needed the chocolate to survive. While they were in the camp, suffering unspeakable horrors with many others, they became friends with a woman named Helene, who like many of those who were taken captive, was pregnant. She was very thin and sickly, so much so that Christophe's mother feared she would not survive labor. So, when the time came for her to deliver, Christophe's mother said to her, "Francine, are you doing all right?" "Yes Mother," she said, "I am managing." "Then if it is OK with you I would like to give our chocolates to Helene because she is giving birth and I am worried that she does not have enough strength. The chocolates will help her." "OK Mother" Christophe said. They gave her the chocolate, Helene survived, and the baby was born. She was so tiny, they kept her wrapped up tightly and she did not cry. It was only when they unwrapped her six months later when the camp was liberated that the baby cried for the first time, as if in that moment she was truly born. Not long after that, the survivors scattered to try to rebuild their lives. But decades later, when a now-aging adult Christophe was lecturing at a conference on how the survivors would have benefitted greatly from being offered psychological counseling after the war, one of the psychiatrists who was scheduled to speak after her stepped up to the podium, turned to Christophe, and said in French, "Before I speak I have a gift for you." Then she handed Christophe a piece of chocolate and said simply, "*Je suis le bebe.* (I am the baby.) Thank you."[45]

---

[45] Interview of Francine Christophe, *"Human the Movie,"* Documentary, directed by Yann Arthus-Bertrand, (New York, 2015, The Bettencourt Schueller Foundation and The Good Planet Foundation, Producers), film clip retrieved May 21, 2016 from https://www.youtube.com/watch?v'gXGfngjmwLA

When Christophe recounted this incident as part of a recent documentary film on Holocaust survivors, her moving story went viral on Facebook, with over 450,000 shares and 7,000 comments. She is now celebrated for her self-sacrifice, as she should be. But she never thought of herself as being special or a hero for giving away the chocolate meant to save her life. She thought of herself as a decent human being. So, on this weekend, when our nation celebrates the heroes who gave their lives to liberate the oppressed and defend freedom in this nation and around the world in too many horrible wars, I have been thinking about what makes someone a hero. Do you think many of the recognized heroes we are remembering this weekend did whatever they did because they were seeking fame and glory? I don't. I think very few true heroes set out to be one, or see themselves as heroes. They just do what they do, whether it is a daring act of self-sacrifice or a small gesture which makes a huge difference because it is the right thing to do in the moment. I've also been thinking about the thousands over the ages who have not been remembered by name. Does the fact that they were forgotten make their acts any less heroic?

It is good that we are honoring both the remembered and the forgotten this weekend, just as it is good that civilians like Francine Christophe are now being honored for their saving acts during times of war. But given that so many of the people who have done the right thing throughout the centuries did so without giving a thought to how they would be recognized, or whether they would be rewarded for their actions, today I think it is also worth recognizing that as much as we love our heroes and are grateful for their actions, the "hero narrative" which is so pervasive in our culture is still problematic. David LaMotte is an international peacemaker, author, speaker and folk singer who recently led a retreat for pastors in Baltimore Presbytery. During the retreat, he summarized the "hero narrative" as one which says our problems will be solved and the world will be saved when an extraordinary individual sweeps in and does something dramatic at a moment of crisis.

We love the hero narrative in our country, as the longtime tradition of summer blockbuster super hero movies testifies. We love the idea of caped-crusaders, or roguish astronauts or fedora-wearing archeologists arriving just in time to save the world from aliens, threatening asteroids, Nazis and more. We love the idea so much that we aren't even picky about who can be our hero. Remember Mighty Mouse? Anyone willing to save the day for the rest of us, even a mouse or an anti-hero will do. This narrative is such a strong part of our culture that right now many Americans are consciously or unconsciously judging the presidential candidates by how readily they think they can single-handedly save our nation, even though it's not the president's job to act singlehandedly, nor his or her responsibility to save the nation or the world.

Now let me say again to be clear: it is never wrong to praise people who do extraordinary things for others. It is never wrong to honor those who make the world a better place through their self-sacrificing service. But as LaMotte observed, the problem with the hero narrative is that it is both unrealistic and generally disempowering.[46] Summer blockbusters do not make us want to be super heroes ourselves. They make us believe that we are nothing like them. They also make us wish for and wait for individual saviors, and can convince us that if there isn't a visible crisis, then a problem isn't serious enough to warrant either our shining the bat signal, or doing something ourselves. In sum, the hero narrative can lead us to conclude there is no problem when there is one, or that it's not "our problem" to fix, instead of inspiring us to reach for the chocolate in our pockets and become part of the solution. LaMotte argued our insufficient response to the problem of climate change is an example of this.

The Bible offers us a very different kind of narrative. Sure, there are lots of heroes in the Bible. There are military heroes like Joshua, David, Deborah and Jael; there are spiritual heroes, like Moses and the prophets and John the Baptist. And of course, in Christ, we have the one true Savior of the world, who is beyond all compare. But the existence of these heroes notwithstanding, the Gospel narrative woven throughout the Old and New Testaments is exactly the opposite of the one that says we can sit back and wait for our Savior to solve the problems in the world. The people of Israel desperately wanted a Savior to do that because they loved the hero narrative as much as we do. But the biblical characters whom we now recognize

---

[46] LaMotte, David, <u>Worldchanging 101: Challenging the Myth of Powerlessness</u> (Montreat: Dryad Pub., 2014), 63-76.

as heroes are the ones who, because of their faith in God, did what they needed to do without waiting for the Messiah to do it for them.

Shiphrah and Puah are two such heroes. According to *the Book of Exodus*, when Pharaoh turned against the Hebrew people, first enslaving them and then trying to eliminate them through genocide, these two midwives refused to follow Pharaoh's orders to kill the newborn males born to Hebrew women. Risking their own lives, they ensured the children would be safely delivered, and then made up an excuse when Pharaoh questioned why male babies still survived. According to some strands of Jewish tradition, these women were not Hebrews themselves; they just wanted to do the right thing. According to other strands, the women were Moses' mother Jochebed, and his sister Miriam, who feared and worshiped Yahweh more than Pharaoh. But whoever they were, they did not wait for a savior to intervene. They did what they could do, which in the end enabled Moses to survive, and changed history forever.

In today's New Testament lesson, we hear of dozens of others who also made a difference, not because they sought recognition, but because they loved Christ and wanted to serve him. In some manuscripts, these early ambassadors of God's love are called the Seventy, in others, the Seventy-two. Both numbers have biblical significance. Seventy elders worked with and for Moses when they were trying to live according to God's commands in the wilderness; and according to *Genesis* 10, seventy-two is the number of nations which were birthed from the descendants of Noah after the flood, a number that represents all the peoples of the world. So, Jesus or Luke could have had either concept in mind when choosing the number. In any case, *Luke* says that after Jesus called the more famous twelve disciples, he called and sent out roughly six dozen other followers to be his ambassadors, by going ahead to nearby villages, healing people, and sharing the good news of God's love.

When they went out to do the work of Christ, the Seventy did not wear capes and masks and shiny red boots. They took so little with them that they were dependent upon the hospitality of those whom they visited. Yet through the grace of God, they were able to do extraordinary acts of healing and transformation. They were even able to cast out evil with the love of God they shared. This surprised and delighted them as much as the people they helped. But when they came back excited to report this to Jesus, he didn't throw them a parade; he didn't even offer the praise we would expect. It's not that he was ungrateful for their work. It's that he wanted to remind them whom they all were called to glorify. They had been able to work wonders because Jesus had empowered them with God's grace. Therefore, their ministry was not about them, it was about God. Their reward would be that their names would be written in heaven, not in the ancient equivalent of a newspaper, or on a plaque on the Temple wall.

We don't know who the Seventy were. A hundred or more years after Christ ascended, leaders in the early Church started making lists of possible candidates. But these lists have been discredited, in part because they mostly name men who were bishops in the Church at the time the lists were written, a convenient form of retroactive credentialing if there ever was one. Scholars know that the Seventy more likely consisted of male and female missionary teams, since we know from Paul's letters and the *Book of Acts* that that is how the Gospel was spread after Pentecost. Husband and wife teams, like Priscilla and Aquila, Mary and Clopas, Andronicus and Junia went forth together to share the good news. They were ordinary folk– some Jewish, some Gentile– who were inspired by God's love in Christ to make their lives about sharing God's grace, following Jesus' way, and doing the right thing. They did this even though doing so sometimes put their lives at risk. They did this even though Jesus was not visibly present with them. They were heroes whose names no one remembers any more.

The difference between the world's hero narrative, and the biblical narrative, according to LaMotte, is that the biblical narrative calls us to ground our sense of purpose in being part of a larger faith community, instead of telling us to wait for a heroic savior.[47] In today's terms, we would say that the biblical narrative affirms the importance of being a part of a movement. The movement of the people of Israel was to witness to the liberating power of God, and to show how obeying God's commandments would bring peace and prosperity to all. Similarly, the movement of the disciples of Christ, known as "the Way," was to witness to the liberating power of God's

---

[47] *Ibid*, Worldchanging 101, 63-76.

grace in Christ. They were to demonstrate how following his Way would bring justice and righteousness and abundant life to all God's children, men and women, Jew and Gentile, instead of just a few, and to overcome evil with good.

Through our baptisms we became a part of this movement. That means that although we affirm that Christ will return some day, we also affirm that we are not supposed to allow problems to fester while we wait for his return. We're called to work to make the kingdom of God more fully realized on earth. We have been sent, like the Seventy, to do his work of healing and transformation here and now by sharing God's love. Like them, we have the Spirit to equip us so we do not need to fear if we cannot leap tall buildings or walk on water. We just need to do what we can do, when the circumstances call for someone to step in.

Only God knows whether some of us here will be given the opportunity to put our lives on the line to ensure justice for the endangered or oppressed like Shiphrah and Puah. But the odds are good that all of us will continue to be given opportunities to make a critical difference in the lives of individuals with a small gesture like Francine Christophe's because we have already shown God that we are good at doing that. Society may not know what we do for decades, if ever. But we do not do what we do in order to get praise or parades. We do what we do because it's the right thing to do, and because even if no one else remembers our names, God will. So, let us give thanks for the heroes who have been recognized, remembering that there were many more who were not, and celebrate the good news each day that in the kingdom of God, every one of us has the power to make a difference in God's name.

I'd like to close today with a video. Although it was created to be a commercial, it captures beautifully some of the many ways we all can be heroes. I could have made a similar video of any number of you, if I followed you around with a camera. But I don't think you would have appreciated that. May the Spirit speak to you through this clip and each day as you are confronted with problems someone needs to help solve. [Video shown.[48]]

---

[48] See TVC Thai Life Insurance, (Apr. 3, 2014)."Unsung Heroes" [Video] Retrieved May 23, 2016, from https://www.youtube.com/watch?v=uaWA2GbcnJU

Christ and the Cosmos: Is Belief in an Immanent God Compatible with Belief in a Multiverse?
Psalm 8; Colossians 1:15-20

Weren't the images from the Hubble Space telescope we saw in the Introit astounding? They are so beautiful, so alien, so huge! Several of us got to see some more of them a couple of months ago at a Forum lunch, and heard more about the way the Hubble is enabling humanity to know more about deep space than ever before, even about the beginning of time and the universe. It's mind-boggling stuff to think about. For example, just to give you a sense of scale, imagine our solar system with its eight planets (or 9 if you are still a Pluto-hold out), were the size of a quarter. If it were, then our galaxy, the Milky Way, which is home to roughly 100 billion solar systems besides our own, would be approximately the size of North America.[49] Now add to that image in your brain the fact that cosmologists estimate that there are between 100 and 500 billion galaxies like the Milky Way in the universe! Who can even imagine a scale so large? Just thinking about it while gazing up at the stars on a clear night is enough to make a person feel awfully small. But for people of faith, the experience can be not just humbling, but also troubling. Where does the God we know in Jesus Christ fit into that vast expanse, and where do we? So, for today's question from our "Faith in the Real-World series," we'll be considering Christ and the cosmos, and the question: "Is belief in an immanent God compatible with belief in a multiverse?"

I'll get to what a multiverse is in a few minutes. But before I do that I want to break today's question into two because people's spiritual troubles with the topic tend to fall into two categories. For some people, the tension between faith and science is a question of

---

[49] *The Night Sky,* "Our Home in the Universe- The Milky Way," by Darrell Heath, UALR University Television, Comcast 61 and Uverse 99, Aug. 2014, Little Rock, retrieved at http://ualr.edu/tv/2014/08/16/august-2014-our-home-in-theuniverse-the-milky-way.

hermeneutics, that is, how we understand and interpret Holy Scripture. "Considering all we know of space from the Hubble, and of the world from a variety of sciences," they wonder, "what are we to make of the creation stories in *Genesis*? Do we have to reject science to be faithful to the Bible and God?" These kinds of questions are easy to answer in our Presbyterian tradition. We do not have to reject the authority of the Bible considering the Big Bang Theory, or Darwin's theory of evolution, or any other scientific theories on the nature of the universe because we recognize that the Bible is not a science authority for us, nor is it attempting to present a scientific record of the beginning of the universe. The Bible is a theological authority for us.

Written more than a thousand years before the Enlightenment, the Creation stories in *Genesis* were created to affirm certain profound and fundamental theological truths about the origin of life, the nature of God, the nature of humanity, and our purpose in the universe. The stories themselves are theological poetry, not science or history. In our Presbyterian tradition, therefore, while we recognize that the description of Creation in *Genesis* is scientifically inaccurate if taken literally, (because it assumes a six-day creation and depicts an ancient Mesopotamian vision of the earth, which included a domed sky with little windows in it so God could make it rain), we also recognize that *Genesis* affirms theological truths which are essential to our faith. It affirms that God created the universe and everything in it including humankind, and called Creation good. It affirms that humankind was made in the image of God for relational living; and it affirms that we were called to serve as God's stewards to care for God's Creation. As I said a few weeks ago, it is the domain of science to address "how things work." It is the domain of faith to address more existential, "Why?" questions. We don't need to disbelieve the lessons of one discipline to believe the lessons of the other, or to compartmentalize the science part of our brains from the faith part.

For progressive Christians who are already comfortable with a scholarly, socio-historical approach to Scripture, however, the problem posed by cosmology is not a hermeneutic one, it's a theological one. Millennia before the Hubble telescope was created the Psalmist summarized the problem when he wrote: "When I look at your heavens, the work of your fingers, the moon and the stars that you have established; what are human beings that you are mindful of them, mortals that you care for them?" As Christians, we believe in a Triune God who is not only the Creator of heaven and earth, but also our Savior and Sustainer. We believe that our God is far more than a giant watchmaker who got things started; through Jesus Christ and the Holy Spirit, God is still deeply invested in our existence here and now, actively involved in our lives, and trying to guide us into a future with hope. The theological word which describes how God is with us in an intimate, relational way is "immanence." But in a universe of 500 billion galaxies, does believing in such an immanent God make rational sense?

To answer this question thoroughly, we'd need a lot more time than we have right now.[50] But for now, here's an abbreviated answer. Modern science and cosmology may keep expanding the size of the known universe, and enhancing our knowledge of it, but these discoveries do not disprove either the existence of God in general, or of an imminent God in particular; just the opposite. There is so much in cosmology that points to the existence of God that atheist scientists who do not want to prove God's existence are having to speculate more and more fantastic theoretical concepts in order to explain how things could possibly work without God.

It all started when Einstein discovered that the universe was most likely finite. He didn't like this idea because if the universe is finite, that means it had a beginning, and if it had a beginning, then that leaves room for the idea that someone began it. So, Einstein added a constant to some of his mathematical equations to get rid of the evidence supporting finiteness.[51] But years later, scientists, not

---

[50] For more information I recommend the following, which I consulted for this sermon: Clayton, Philip, God and Contemporary Science (Grand Rapids: Wm. B. Eerdmans Pub. Co., 1997); The Church and Contemporary Cosmology, James B. Miller & Kenneth E. McCall Eds. (Pittsburgh: Carnegie Melon Univ. Press, 1990); Davies, Paul, God and the New Physics (New York: Simon & Schuster Inc., 1983); Kaku, Michio, Parallel Worlds: A Journey Through Creation, Higher Dimensions, and the Future of the Cosmos (New York: Anchor Books, 2005); and Worthing, Mark William, God, Creation, and Contemporary Physics (Minneapolis: Fortress Press,1996).

[51] See e.g. Aczel, Amir, *"Einstein's Lost Theory Describes a Universe Without a Big Bang,"* DISCOVER MAGAZINE, Mar. 7, 2014, retrieved from

realizing his motivation, proved his constant was incorrect, and ended up making the Big Bang Theory the dominant theory of how our universe began. As soon as this theory was in play, it became clear that there was room for God not just at the beginning, but thereafter as well.

You see, as physicists tried to calculate everything that happened after "the Bang," they discovered that at every level of the universe, from the atomic, to the galactic, to the cosmic, there is evidence of what scientists now call stunning and surprising "fine-tuning."[52] On the screens behind me are only some of the dozens of the mathematical constants which are essential to our universe, but which should not have been able to be, either because having the circumstances to arrive at them was a long shot in the extreme, or because they can function only within an extremely narrow range of precision to work.[53] For example, from the moment the universe

---

http://blogs.discovermagazine.com/crux/2014/03/07/einsteins-lost-theory-describes-a-universe-without-a-big-bang/#.V3ZuRqI6eSp. Einstein's constant was known as the "cosmological constant."

[52] See *God: New Evidence*, *"John Polkinghorne talks about evidence of God from fine tuning,"* produced by www.focus.org.uk, YouTube video, posted Jan. 26, 2010, retrieved from http://www.focus.org.uk/polkinghorne.php. See also Worthing, God, Creation, and Contemporary Physics, 43-47.

[53] Ross, Dr. Hugh, *"Reasons to Believe: Design and the Anthropic Principle,"* RTB 30, Jan. 1, 1989, retrieved from http://www.reasons.org/articles/design-and-theanthropic-principle: These support the argument of intelligent design:
- the gravitational coupling constant
- the strong nuclear force coupling constant
- the weak nuclear force coupling constant
- the electromagnetic coupling constant
- the ratio of electron to proton mass
- the age of the universe
- the expansion rate of the universe
- the entropy level of the universe
- the mass of the universe
- the uniformity of the universe
- the stability rate of protons
- the nuclear resonance energy levels of beryllium, carbon and oxygen
- the location of our sun in the galaxy
- the density of our sun
- the earth's distance from the sun
- the moon's distance from the earth
- the tilt of the earth's axis
- the composition of our atmosphere
- the seismic activity of our planet

God in the Here and Now

began, it should not have been able to create stars or galaxies, but it did.

If we zoom from the universe to our galaxy, the evidence keeps piling up. As you can see from this slide, our sun is more than two-thirds of the way out from the center of the galaxy.

If it had been a smidgen closer in or further out, we wouldn't have had the stability to have our solar system. If the sun hadn't been denser than most stars, if the earth hadn't been where it is in relation to the sun, if the moon hadn't been where it is in relation to the earth, and so on and so on, science says we would not be here today. As a result, many scientists from physicists to physicians have observed that the universe seems to be inexplicably, yet uniquely designed to produce human beings against astronomical odds. Scientists call this observation "the anthropic principle.[54] Basically, God's fingerprints are everywhere, which is why so many physicists and cosmologists who spend their days gazing at the vast incomprehensible expanses of space, are also believers in God.

Not all scientists are believers, however, which is where the multiverse idea came from. Did you ever see the old *Twilight Zone* episode when an astronaut lands on earth only to discover that he has accidentally landed in a parallel universe?[55] The earth he landed on still had his wife and his house and his job in it. But all kinds of little

---

[54] Ibid. See also *"Evidence of the Design of the Universe through the Anthropic Principle,"* IDEA- Intelligent Design and Evolution Awareness Center, retrieved from http://www.ideacenter.org/contentmgr/showdetails.php/id/837

[55] See Serling Rod, The Twilight Zone, *"The Parallel,"* (TV Episode directed by Alan Crossland Jr.), Mar. 14, 1963, retrieved from http://www.imdb.com/title/tt04670

things were off. He thought he was going mad until he realized he was on earth in a parallel universe. Well that sci-fi premise is now a popular and legitimate cosmological theory. In order to get God out of the equation, yet still explain why the cosmos and quantum particles act the way they do, some scientists are now arguing that we must live in a "multiverse:" an infinite series of parallel universes in which all conceivable choices and variables play out. Ours just happened to be the one in which the variables ended up favorable for human life. But they ended up that way by chance. The common illustration given to support this hypothesis is that if you gave an infinite number of monkeys with typewriters an infinite amount of time, one of them eventually would write the works of Shakespeare.

John Polkinghorne, who is both a physicist and an Anglican priest, thinks this idea and its logic is ridiculous. Even if it were conceivably true that a monkey could produce Shakespeare, he said, to conclude when one finds a Shakespearean play, that it must have been written by one of an infinite number of monkeys instead of by Shakespeare, is absurd. There is no evidence of a multiverse; there is an abundance of evidence of divine design. Science is supposed to consider the simplest possible explanation as the most likely, not the most far-fetched. [56]Even if we do live in a multiverse, as Polkinghorne notes, that scenario does not get rid of the need for God or eliminate the possibility of God. There are an infinite number of even numbers in the universe, but if what was needed to produce human life was an odd number, then you'd still be stuck. All the strongest evidence points to God. So to speculate otherwise, is to dress up belief in the guise of science.[57]

As those who do believe in God, we do not need to do such mental gymnastics to avoid the obvious conclusion. All we need to do is figure out how to get from God as Creator, to God in Christ; and the Bible does that for us. As today's lesson from *Colossians* affirms, Christ is the image of the invisible God, and by him all things in heaven and on earth, both visible and invisible were created. The Cosmic Sovereign whom the Psalmist praised, and Christ, are one and the same. Christ came in part, so that when we look at the stars which were so carefully

---

[56] This principle is called "Occam's Razor."
[57] *Ibid*, God: New Evidence, "*John Polkinghorne talks about evidence of God from fine tuning.*"

crafted by God to produce us, we would not worship the stars, but would worship the one who created them. Christ came, in part, so that we would be able to have an intimate relationship with a God whose vastness and power would otherwise be beyond our comprehension. Christ came so that we would know that God expects us to make our invisible God's reign on earth visible, and so that we would know the precise parameters which will enable us and our world to thrive, instead of collapsing or exploding. Jesus is the divine constant that we need in order to balance the equation for our lives in a way that the sum of God's good creation and our work equals peace, justice, and love for all.

The blessing of cosmology, besides its being intellectually stimulating, is that by pointing out the vastness and the complexity of the universe, it humbles us. We need to feel more humble to mitigate the fact that human beings think so highly of ourselves, our intelligence, and our powers, that we are more inclined to create God in our image than we are to worship the real God, whose intelligence, will, power and presence are on a scale we will never fully understand, let alone control. We like to put ourselves on pedestals and God in a box. So, it is a good thing that cosmology reminds us of our finiteness, our vulnerability, and our constant need to learn more. But there is more to us than our cosmic smallness, which is why we also need faith.

Among the many blessings of Christianity, is that it reminds us that even in our tiny, relative powerlessness, we matter and are not alone. The God who made the heavens and earth, and who may have made an infinite number of universes and aliens for all we know, is also the God who made us out of love and a desire for a relationship with us. That great God, our Creator, then came as Christ into our tiny, vulnerable existence so that we would know that God is not too big to care, and not too far to help. Christ came so that we would do more than look for God's fingerprints in space; we would also look for God's signature on our hearts. Without Christ, we might not know the formula for a future with hope. We might not appreciate the sustaining and saving power of love. We need to understand Christ, not just the cosmos, if we want to know our own beginnings and who we were made to be.

While some cosmologists and quantum physicists have been pursuing the idea of a multiverse in order to explain how our universe works against so many inexplicable odds, another physicist, named Fotini Kalamara, has developed a way to connect Einstein's relativity with quantum theory without the need of a hypothetical multiverse or an infinite number of monkeys.[58] I can't begin to explain to you her theory because I am not a physicist. All I know is that it has something to do with light cones and spin networks. But what interests me about her theory is that when she first came up with it, she hit a wall because it seemed to prove that you needed someone outside of the universe in order to observe it to make it real. That would suggest God again, which she didn't want to do. Then she crunched some numbers and found that her theory could work if creatures inside the universe could observe how light illuminated their slice of the universe. "We can still construct a meaningful portrait of the Universe based on the partial information we each receive" she said. I'm not sure she realizes it, but either way she has made a case for God. Our faith in a Triune God, Creator, Redeemer and Sustainer helps us to see that. As the Bible reminds us, we have a transcendent God who made the universe and therefore is outside of it. But we also have an immanent God, who even now, is gazing at the stars with us, and shining light on our own small corner of the cosmos, so that in addition to having a meaningful portrait of the universe, we can also have a meaningful portrait of its Creator, and who we were made to be. Thanks be to God! Amen.

---

[58] See Gefter, Amanda, *"Throwing Einstein for a Loop,"* SCIENTIFIC AMERICAN, Dec. 2002, archived at http://www.stealthskater.com/Documents/Kalamara1.pdf

The Way in the World
Amos 9:5-7; John 14:1-7

Last week we considered the Christian call to be ambassadors of reconciliation, a calling which flows from our having embraced the saving gift of God's grace in Christ. Just as God has overcome the estrangement that existed between humanity and God with love and grace, so we are called to work to overcome the estrangement that exists between human beings. That is a huge and difficult task because as the news keeps reminding us, human beings these days especially, are more divided than ever before. We distinguish and distance ourselves from others in every conceivable way, based upon race, gender and differences in our wealth, nationality, culture and politics. But perhaps the saddest basis for division, given that we are called to do God's work, is religion. Right now, there are something like 4,300 different religions in the world according to a recent estimate. Think about that! That's a lot of division, and it doesn't even count the rising numbers of people we're estranged from because they do not believe in any god. The two biggest religions are Christianity and Islam. Yet as we all know, we two are far from allied; and now because of the violent acts of fanatics, certain politicians are encouraging us to turn against each other even more. If the two biggest religions cannot move beyond self-righteous suspicion, and stand together against divisiveness and persecution in the name of God, how on earth are we going to bring together all the other kinds of believers? So, today's Faith in the Real-World question is: In today's pluralistic world, how should we, who are called to be ambassadors of reconciliation, see and relate to people of other religions, given the verse "I am the way and the truth and the life. No one comes to the Father except through me?"

Before I can answer this question, I have to offer one sad disclaimer. I can answer the question only from the perspective of Reformed Protestants in the Presbyterian Church (USA) because Christians themselves are so divided that it is impossible right now to speak accurately on behalf of all Christians. I can't even speak accurately on behalf of all people who are called Presbyterians. I pray by God's grace that this won't always be the case!

In any case, in our denomination we recognize that there are many texts in the Bible which offer helpful insight as we strive to think about people of other religions. For example, Paul's inclusive statement from *Romans* 5: "Therefore just as one man's trespass led to condemnation *for all*, so one man's act of righteousness leads to justification and life *for all;*" or his assurance to the Galatians, "There is no longer Jew or Greek, there is no longer slave or free, there is no longer male and female for all of you are one in Christ Jesus," are both great places to begin a ministry of reconciliation because they are bridge-building texts. (Rom. 5:18; Gal. 3:28). John 14:6, on the other hand, is not such a helpful text because the language "No one comes to the Father except through me," pretty much encourages people to build walls instead of bridges. For this reason, one author I read called it a "clobber text" used by Christians who want to point out who is "in" and beloved to God, and who is "out" and going to hell.[59] "It's Jesus' way or the highway" the text seems to say.

For Christians raised in strong evangelical or fundamentalist traditions, this text, paired with John 3:16, summarizes the Gospel in a nutshell: "Choose Christ and be saved, or reject Christ and be condemned." Therefore, they see their call to reconciliation as a call to try to convert people to Christ in order that they will be saved. But for those of us who are not as comfortable condemning the rest of the world to hell, or worshiping a God who would do that, it is hard to know what to make of this text. We don't want to ignore something from the Bible that Jesus said; but we don't want to believe that it says what it seems to say either.

Fortunately, we don't have to because many scholars believe that the text does not actually mean what people usually think it means. When you consider the social, literary and historical context of the text, as we in our tradition believe one must do in order to discern and honor God's word properly, it becomes evident that this verse was not written to justify the practice of condemning Muslims, Jews or anyone else to hell. Islam didn't even exist then. The text was

---

[59] Gockel, Rev. Stan, *"Is Jesus a Way or THE WAY?"* a sermon deliver at Bellbrook Presbyterian Church, May 22, 2011.

written to speak solely to Christians and offer guidance as to how we can stay close to God in this life and the next.

Just who was offering this guidance is subject to debate. A good number of scholars believe that Jesus himself didn't say these words, but that John did. One of the reasons for this is that John's gospel was written so much later than the other three, around 70 years after Christ's Ascension. By that time, people's memories of what Jesus said were more than a little bit fuzzy. Also, by the time it was written, John was not interested in recording a factual account of Jesus' life and teachings; that had been done already lots of times. John was interested in writing a theological advocacy piece which would explain who Jesus was, and why people should follow him even though he had not returned as expected, and the kingdom he proclaimed had not yet come. John knew that people needed to hear his answers because the Christian Church at that time was enduring during a gut-wrenching and bewildering spiritual divorce. The Jewish synagogues were kicking Christian out for preaching the Gospel. This was not the same situation as my telling someone he mustn't come to Prince of Peace anymore and encouraging him to go to a different church. This was more like Amish shunning. To be kicked out of the synagogue had profound social and economic implications as well as spiritual ones for the Christians, especially when Christians were also increasingly being persecuted by Rome. So, a lot of believers were wondering if professing faith in Jesus was such a good idea after all.

In writing his gospel, John wanted to do more than tell the people that Jesus was the way to heaven. He believed in something called "realized eschatology" which means he believed that one was saved not just for the next life, but for this one too. So even though we know that John believed that Jesus came to save the entire world because he says in 3:17, "Indeed, God did not send the Son into the world to condemn the world, but in order that the world might be saved through him," and even though John recorded that Jesus said that he had "other sheep" which he would bring into in his flock, a lot of John's gospel still pushes the importance of believing in Christ in order to dwell in the kingdom of God now. His audience was losing their faith. So, some scholars think he had Jesus offer his "I am the way" speech to encourage them to remain faithful. He wasn't speaking about whether one could or could not be saved by world religions. He was speaking about the fact that one *could* be saved through Jesus Christ. He was speaking to the importance of staying true to Christ and following his way as the way to dwell with God in this life.

Not all scholars think the famous words were John's, however. Some still believe Jesus spoke them. For those scholars, the key to understanding them lies in recognizing that they were part of the parting instructions Jesus gave his disciples right before he died. "Do not let your hearts be troubled," he said, offering pastoral care to his own disciples, not judgment to a mixed faith crowd. "I am going to prepare a place for you... and you know the way I am going." "No we don't!" Thomas said, always the one willing to say what the others were thinking but afraid to say. So, Jesus said *to him* specifically, "I am the way, the truth and the life. No one comes to the Father except through me."

Why would Jesus say this? It is clear from the story that Thomas wasn't asking a world religions question in that moment, his question was far more personal. He was really asking, "But what do I do when you're gone Jesus? What do I have to do, where do I have to go, how will I find God and know that I'm OK with God without you?" In other words, he was freaking out about Jesus' departure and thus began worrying about what he had to do to please God, instead of celebrating what Jesus had just told him God was about to do for him. "I don't know" Thomas said in a panic. "I don't know the way to get in!" Jesus sensed all of this, so he said "Thomas, take a deep breath. I am the way you and all of humanity are being saved. I've got that covered. No one is going to be saved by doing stuff themselves. They are going to be saved because of what I am about to do. I am the way, not you. What I've taught you about God's grace and love is true and will keep you close to me even after you can't see me. So, don't panic. Just keep doing what we've been doing together after I'm gone."

People who use this passage as a weapon, tend to take it out of the context of this loaded good-bye moment and treat it as if Jesus was addressing the UN or a world religions conference. But to use this text to justify the position that one must make a profession of faith in Christ or one won't be saved, is to advocate exactly the opposite of what Jesus was trying to teach in that moment. He wasn't saying, "After I'm gone only those who say the sinner's prayer will get in," or, "Just remember, Thomas, that my name is the secret password if you want to get into heaven." He was saying that he was going to be how humanity would be saved. In other words, the statement is specific in that it names Jesus as the means by which humanity would be reconciled to God, but it is not exclusive because it does not say only people who profess faith in Christ will be reconciled.

The Old Testament lesson today helps us to understand this distinction better. The people of Israel are called God's "chosen people" throughout the Old Testament. That sounds very exclusive. But as the prophets tried to make clear again and again, the fact that the Jews were chosen to be a people who would teach the world about God's love did not mean that God did not love or had rejected the rest of the world. It meant that they had been given a job. So, when Israel got on its high horse about its special relationship, while at the same time failing to do the job God had given them, God, through Amos, cut them down to size by pointing out that while their calling was unique and specific, their having a saving relationship with God was not. "Are you not like the Ethiopians to me, O people of Israel? Did I not bring Israel up from the land of Egypt and the Philistines from Caphtor and the Arameans from Kir?" The Ethiopians, (or the Cushites in the Hebrew), were looked down upon by the Israelites, even though Moses married a Cushite woman. They lived in the Sinai Peninsula. Today we would call them Arabs. The Philistines were the enemy of Israel – remember the story of David and Goliath? And the Arameans were the people Abraham and Sarah left behind to go off following God, people who lived in what we would now call Iraq. So, God was basically saying, "You know all those people you look down upon because you think you're special because I called you and I liberated you from Egypt? Guess what? I liberated them too. Yes, I have provided different exodus narratives to all your enemies. I brought up the Philistines from captivity in Caphtor, and the Arameans from captivity in Kir. I am in the business of setting people free. You are special to me, but so are they. So, don't get the idea that because you were chosen they have been rejected. I have saved them from other things, and chosen them for other things."

The Old Testament is filled with stories of God using outsiders and nonbelievers to further God's plan. Ruth the Moabite and Rahab the Canaanite are part of Jesus' genealogy. Cyrus of Persia is even called God's "messiah." The reason we have a hard time remembering this is that we, like most human beings, still want the salvation narrative to be about us and our merit, not about God's grace. But in both the Old and the New Testament, the salvation narrative is about God, and God's willingness to love, forgive, liberate, and save us even though we haven't done anything to merit such gifts. Recognizing this is the first step toward our being able to be reconciled with our neighbors.

The second step, as theologian Miroslav Volf learned the hard way from living through the genocide and warfare between Bosnia and Croatia, is then for us to appreciate that there is a difference between reconciliation and conversion.[60] People confuse the concepts all the time. So, we try very hard to get "the others" to believe what we believe in the name of reconciliation because we think then the world will be saved. But since God does the saving not us, true Christian reconciliation is about embracing "the other" as equally beloved and valuable even though he or she is and always will be different from us. It's not demanding conversion to our beliefs; it's about working to find common ground because we know they have been saved by our loving and liberating God as much as we have.

As Marcus Borg has noted, in the statement "I am the way and the truth and the life," Jesus and/or John showed us where to find that common ground. It's not in a set of doctrines or beliefs; it's in "the Way" that Jesus embodied, the truth he revealed about God's love for all people, and the gift of new life he wanted so badly for us to accept.[61] Like Thomas, we "know the way" if we only stop to think about it. The way of Christ is a way defined by love and grace and forgiveness. The way of Christ is a way which celebrates generosity and humble servanthood, not seeking material reward or power over others. The way of Christ is a way which affirms the importance of loving your neighbor as yourself, showing hospitality to the stranger, and recognizing all of humanity's need for God. It is a way of rebirth and re-creation in God's grace. Islam, Judaism, Buddhism, Hinduism, and I would bet all the rest of the thousands of other religions, all

---

[60] See Volf, Miroslav, Exclusion & Embrace: A Theological Exploration of Identity, Otherness, and Reconciliation (Nashville: Abingdon Press, 1996), 109-110.

[61] Borg, Marcus, *"Jesus: The Way, the Truth, the Life"* Belief.net article, Aug. 2000, retrieved July 12, 2016 at
http://www.beliefnet.com/faiths/christianity/2000/08/jesus-the-way-the-truth-the-life

celebrate this way, although they call it by different names. Thus, a Hindu professor who came to preach at a Christian seminary where Borg worked could say as a faithful Hindu, after choosing John 14:6 as his preaching text, "This verse is absolutely true. Jesus is the only way.... And that way– of dying to an old way of being and being born into a new way of being– is known in all the religions of the world. The way of Jesus is a universal way, known even to the millions who have never heard of Jesus."[62] We all know the way, we just don't follow it. If we did, even in our diversity we would be allies, not enemies.

So, where then does that leave us? In 2002 our denomination summarized our stance on people of other faiths in a document called *"Hope in the Lord Jesus Christ."*[63] The document affirms our profession of faith, that Jesus was the Christ; he was God and Love incarnate. But it then goes on to address other religions in a very gracious way, basically saying, "We testify that we are saved through Christ, not by anything that we do or did. We also testify that since our salvation is not of our own doing and was undeserved, we cannot possibly say with certainty what God wants to do with people of other faiths or non-believers. We must remain agnostic about their salvation because it's not our business. But based upon everything we know of God's saving ways in Christ, and of God's love for all people, we can say that we have every reason to be optimistic for them."

This document helps us to see how we can fulfill our Christian callings to testify to Jesus Christ and be ambassadors of reconciliation at the same time. We simply need to be specific but not exclusive. We speak to the way and the truth and the life we receive through the grace of God in Jesus Christ. We encourage people to embrace the Way because it is the way to joy and peace in this life as well as the next. But we do so with humility, knowing that God's way will already have been revealed somehow to the people of other faiths with whom we speak because God is in the liberating business. We strive not to save one another, but to connect with one another because we have learned through our Savior, Jesus Christ, that God's new creation will not be

---

[62] *Ibid.*

[63] *"Hope in the Lord Jesus Christ,"* A Position Paper of the Office of Theology and Worship of the Presbyterian Church (U.S.A.), 2002, retrieved from http://www.pcusa.org/search/?criteria'hope+in+the+lord+jesus+christ

complete until all who have been reconciled by God's grace, are also reconciled with each other. Amen.

God on the Go
Genesis 11:27- 12:9; Matthew 8:18-22

"*Lech Lecha!*" God said to Abram and Sarai, "Go, go out!" in Hebrew; and according to the story that's just what they did. They packed up their belongings and household and went. Although I have talked about Abraham and Sarah before, I wanted us to revisit the famous story again today because you cannot kick off a series on the essential narrative of the Old Testament, which I am doing today, without this story. This is where the story of God's involvement with humanity begins in the Bible. All the stories which come before it -- the story of Adam and Eve, Noah, the Tower of Babel and such -- were added to the Hebrew Scriptures years after this one, to extend the story of the God, which the Jews knew through Abram, back to Creation. That's why they are called "prehistory." But today's story is the beginning for Jews, Christians and Muslims because God's covenant with Abraham marks the beginning of our spiritual ancestors' intentional journey with God. God promised Abraham, "If you go where I will lead you, I will bless you and make you a blessing for others. I will make from you a great nation; and in you all the families of the earth shall be blessed." Abraham and Sarah went as they were commanded, and the rest, as they say, is history. Well specifically, it is theological history. We do not know whether there ever were actual people called Abraham and Sarah or if they are symbolic representatives of an entire historic people known as the 'Aipru, who traveled across the Fertile Crescent, and forever changed the world with their ways and their faith. But either way, this story is jammed packed with all kinds of theological truths which are foundational to our faith and the history of the Church.

Genesis tells us that Abraham and Sarah, (who were known as Abram and Sarai at this point, but I'm going to call them by their more familiar names for simplicity's sake), began their journey with Yahweh in Haran, which was in northern Mesopotamia. Their traveling days started much earlier and further away, however, in a city called Ur, which would be in modern day Kuwait. Abraham grew up there with his father, two brothers, and their families. Ur was where Abraham learned his trade, fell in love and got married. Ur was all he knew for most of his life. But at some point, possibly because one of Abraham's brothers, Haran, died, Abraham's father, Terah, decided to pack up most of the family and leave Ur forever. He took them on the road and did not settle down until they had crossed 600 miles to a city that shared his deceased son's name. So, Abraham already knew what it was like to leave everything familiar behind and live like a nomad before God told him to leave Haran. Whether that made it easier or harder for him to say "yes" is anyone's guess. I would think the latter. But one of the important lessons this story conveys is that Abraham's journey with God was not grounded only in a promise of blessings, it was also grounded in a promise of lots of travel.

Even I didn't appreciate how much travel until I saw his journey in chart form. This chart summarizes his many moves. [Slide shown][64] After that first 600-mile trek from Ur to Haran, Abraham and Sarah then went from Haran to Shechem, another 400 miles. Then they traveled from there to Bethel, just a quick trip at 20 miles, then from Bethel to Egypt 225 miles, and from Egypt back to Bethel. Then they went 35 miles from Bethel to Hebron (known as Mamre), and finally 160 miles from Hebron to Hobah. That is a total of one thousand six hundred and sixty-five miles (if you start in Ur), all done before any motored vehicles were invented! They never knew how far they were going, how long they were going to stay or when God's promises would come true. When they signed on to serve Yahweh, they signed on to move, in much the same way that people in the military today do. They went when God said go, and stayed when God said stay. It was not up to them, but up to God.

The distances they covered alone are enough to make their story remarkable. But when you also consider the ages Abraham and Sarah were when they began their journey with Yahweh, then the story moves from remarkable to thought-provoking. *Genesis* says that Abraham was 75 when he first set out from Haran. Now admittedly, the biblical ages recorded in this part of *Genesis* are biologically unrealistic, so we must take that number with a huge grain of salt. But even so, the literary point being made is that Abraham and Sarah were not newlyweds eager to make their way in the world. They were not like the young fishermen whom Jesus called to follow him, who were

---

[64] See *"Journey of Abraham Part I"*, Barnes' Bible Charts, retrieved Sept. 6, 2016 from http://www.biblecharts.org/oldtestament/journeysofabrahamone.pdf

most likely in their 20s and 30s. Abraham and Sarah were old enough to be thinking more about retirement than adventure. Especially considering how far they already traveled with Terah, no one would have been surprised if they had said, "Sorry but I'm too old for that kind of thing now God. Please pick someone else," or "Thanks for the offer, but I've already experienced more than enough change for my life time. I am done. It's time for the next generation to take over." I doubt anyone would have thought the less of them if they had wanted to sit on their porch in Haran and talk about the golden days back in Ur, rather than head out toward who knows where, with an invisible God who offered no introduction, and who didn't even give them a burning bush to motivate them before sending them into the unknown after an impossible dream. I don't need to tell you all here about the fatigue that comes with age. But Abraham and Sarah did not say "no thank you" despite their age. Something in them, or in the voice of God, or the promise made them willing to embrace a radical new beginning and a life of constant movement at the very time they should have been preparing for their ending in one place.

Whatever it was that made them go, their decision changed history forever. Through their journey, they introduced the world to a God unlike all the others, a God whose name is a verb and whose passion is leading people into new and better futures. We see that God again in today's New Testament lesson. The Lectionary skips over this lesson because it doesn't make Jesus look very good. He comes across as more crabby and unsympathetic than patient and loving. But scholars say that that very fact makes it more likely that Jesus did say these things, so we cannot simply ignore the passage because it makes us uncomfortable. Moreover, if you listen to what he says with the Abraham story in your mind, then it sounds more like a statement of the truth than an attempt to be mean. "Foxes have holes, and birds of the air have nests, but the Son of Man has nowhere to lay his head," Jesus said. He was on the move, and he wanted all who wanted to follow him to know that to do so, they would have to be willing to live on the move too. There would be no cushy jobs in palaces waiting for them in Jerusalem in their future with Christ. He couldn't even promise them they would have a shack in Galilee where they could live out their lives in peace. To follow Christ was to embrace a peripatetic lifestyle, a continuous journey with God, doing ministry on the go.

But what about the people who wanted to say "Yes"? Why was Jesus so rude to the man who said he would go wherever Jesus went, or to the man who just wanted to bury his father before he left? There are several ways to interpret his responses. The first interpretation argues that this text simply records Jesus having a bad day. He could see the cross in his future, and was frustrated both by the antagonism of the religious authorities, and the cluelessness of his disciples. He knew the first man would not go to the cross with him. He knew his own disciples would not either. So, he lost his patience. This text reminds us that Jesus was human as well as divine. He experienced irritability and fatigue with the best of us.

Another interpretation focuses on the second man who wanted to bury his father. In Jewish custom, a burial had to be on the same day as the death. But the burial process was a long one to complete. First there was a 7-day grieving period called "sitting Shiva." Then there was a one-year period in which the family waited for the body to decompose on a shelf in a tomb. After a year, the tomb was then opened and the bones collected to be put in an ossuary box to be kept with other ancestors' bones. So even if the man's father had died that day, it could have been that Jesus was saying he didn't have a week or a year to hang around. He knew his time on earth was very limited and needed to get going.

But I like Old Testament scholar Walter Brueggemann's interpretation best.[65] He said that Jesus was not being rude; he was using classic rabbinic hyperbole to convey that when God offers you new life, you should not choose to remain with death. If we want to travel with God, we must commit to God fully, which means we cannot spend our energy and keep our focus on the past, on ways of being that are now done and over. We must not cling to our past failures or successes, to old memories, practices, hurts or fears, but must unload them in order "to travel forward in light obedience with God."[66] God is relentlessly forward-looking, and we must be too, if we want to stay

---

[65] Brueggemann, Walter, *"The Stunning Outcome of a One-Person Search Committee"* in THE JOURNAL FOR PREACHERS, Vol. 25, No. 1, Advent 2001, 36-40.

[66] *Ibid*, 39-40.

in step with the One who alone can bless us and make us a blessing for others in the process.

This is an important lesson for us all to consider when it comes to how we journey individually with God; but it is even more critical now for the Church to learn if it is to continue to walk in step with God into the future. If the old ways of doing Church matter more to us that being with God, we will not be able to follow God because God is doing a new thing. We all know this, whether we want to admit it or not. We can see it and feel it. The changes may seem scary, painful, and sad; but the reality is that the Church, and I mean not just our church, but the Church universal, does not have the same role in society that it used to. It does not hold the same authority or engage people to the same degree that it used to. The distractions of our world now are too many, and the competition too steep. So, the Spirit of God is at work leading people to convey the Gospel in new ways. These ways do not feel like "church" to many of us. But if we want to continue to abide with God and not just with one another, we will still need to let go of whatever keeps us from following where God is now leading. To cling to the past now, either out of fondness for it or fear of the future, is to choose a way that leads to death.

This week I posted on Facebook an article by Bill Wilson called, *"Are we a movement or a program?"* which addresses this problem. I hope you had a chance to read it. Wilson argues that the solution to the Church's problem today is for us to rediscover Christianity as a movement.[67] I mean "movement" in both senses of the word. We must be ready to move– to step out of our comfort zones spiritually, emotionally and physically-- away from old programs and practices, even sometimes from beloved church buildings, to go out into the world, because very few people are going to come in to find us or God anymore. We must recognize, Wilson argues, that although we look back on the 1960s with yearning because those days seemed to be the golden days of the Church, that decade actually marked the beginning of the end of the programmatic era of the Church. Society began changing then and has continued to change so much that the world is fundamentally different

---

[67] Wilson, Bill, *"Are we a movement or a program?"* CENTER FOR HEALTHY CHURCHES, Aug. 20, 2016, available at http://chchurches.org/are-we-a-movement-or-a-program

now for doing ministry than it was then. So, we cannot do what we did then and achieve the same results.

This is a hard truth for most of us to accept because most of us are here love the old ways. But if we think of Christianity as "a movement" in the second sense of that word as well, that is, as a cause, then the truth gets easier to embrace. Think of some of the great movements that have taken place in American history alone– the Boston Tea Party, the Women's Suffrage Movement, the Civil Rights Movement. These were exciting and dynamic movements. People stepped up in those movements to fight against oppression. They fought for all people being valued, and worked for liberation and change for good. These are things worth fighting for! These are Gospel values! Christianity was always meant to be a movement like these. Jesus did not set out to set up an institution, he set out to inspire people to work for the Kingdom of God on earth: to love their neighbors, to challenge injustice, to be instruments of transformation. The first disciples did this, fighting against the oppression of the Empire, breaking down boundaries which exclude and harm. But when Constantine made Christianity the religion of the Empire, the Gospel was domesticated and the movement restructured into a "religion." It was brought inside, and faith became about doing programs and accepting doctrines, more than changing the world.

Now as those old ways are falling out of favor with many, the idea of Christianity as a movement is regaining favor within the Church. This is a good thing because as Wilson put it, "Movement thinking is driven by passion, rather than obligation, fueled by a personal sense of call, focused on a goal and marked by collaborative efforts." It says "no" to rhetoric, policies and people which distract from the goal, and yes to new ideas which allow the Gospel to grow in organic and exciting ways.[68] In other words, movement thinking is perfect for the way people think and operate today. It's hard to persuade the younger generations that being members of a group that meets regularly in a building for worship and fellowship is the best way either to experience God or to change the world. But it isn't hard to persuade them to join movements that are working for good. They want to be

---

[68] *Ibid*, Bill Wilson.

where the action is. They want to make a difference combating racism and sexism, persecution and poverty.

This means that all we must do is to demonstrate that the Church is the headquarters for a movement which offers more than the others. It promises not just blessings for us and for others through us, but also a chance to walk forward each day with God. Do you believe this? As we kick off the new program year, I hope that you will spend some time this year examining what the purpose of Christianity is to you. What part of the movement are you most passionate about, and how do you share that passion with others in the world? If you do this, then letting go will hurt less, and the possibilities for the future become more exciting.

"Do not linger in the past," Jesus told his would be follower. "I know that you loved your Father. I know that you want to honor him. But to love and honor *my* Father is to leave what is past and to walk with me into the future and new life." Right now, God is extending to all this same invitation. The good news is that none of us is too old to accept. But the even better news for us is that whenever God says, "*Lech Lecha*!", "Go, Go out!", we can trust that however long the journey will be and however far we must travel, God will be with us, and will always show us the way. Thanks be to God. Amen.

According to the Deer of the Dawn
Psalm 22; Lamentations 3:19-24

"My God, my God, why have you forsaken me?" What do you think of when you hear those words? If you're like most Christians, your thoughts do not leap immediately to the 22nd Psalm, our Lectionary text for today. They leap instead to the foot of the cross and the image in *Matthew* and *Mark* of a battered, beaten Jesus crying out these words with his last dying breath. These are haunting words of despair and pain, bewilderment and betrayal for most Christians, words we'd rather not think about for very long because they make us feel guilty and sad. But there is reason to believe that Jesus' words may have provoked a very different reaction in the minds and hearts of his early followers. Some of them may have heard in his lamenting cry an unspoken but powerful proclamation of faith; others when they heard him, might even have wondered if Jesus was perhaps trying to telegraph to them one last important lesson in faithfulness from the cross. Some theologians believe that he was. It's a lesson we need to hear now just as much as they did then. But for us to hear the good news implicitly promised in Jesus' poignant plea, we first must recognize what his followers did, that Jesus' words were not his own; they were the opening line of the 22nd Psalm. We also need to rediscover the spiritual practice this psalm affirms, one that his Jewish followers understood well but modern Christians have mostly lost. We need to rediscover the power and purpose of lamenting.

In our day and age, you don't hear much talk about lamenting. What you hear is a lot of complaining because complaining is a big part of our culture. We complain about little things– the weather, the food, the traffic, the time it takes for us to connect to the Internet, the lack of decent shows on T.V. We also complain about big, important things– about the state of the economy, the illnesses and injuries which plague us, the inadequacies of our relationships, the loss of our loved ones, the unfairness of life. Complaining can be very cathartic, which is one reason why we all do it; it can also be community-building. We trade complaints in regular conversation as a way of finding things in common with others. Have you noticed that? "You have ragweed allergies? So do I! I'm practically coughing up my lungs these days..." But whether our complaints are well-warranted or frivolous, simply conversational or born of deeply heart-felt hurts, they usually share one thing in common, and that is that they are focused on us. Life, in some respect, has let us down, hurt us, or simply failed to please. The world should meet our needs and expectations better per our vision; it should be as we want it and need it to be.

The self-focused nature of our complaining makes the practice of complaining a double-edged sword for us. It can make you feel much better, but if you do it a lot, complaining can also make you feel much worse. The more you focus on your own pain, on your own mistakes and injuries, frustrations and needs, the harder it becomes to focus on anything else. What starts as passing dissatisfaction can become lasting depression. What starts as a form of release, can become a trap. The psychological term for this is ruminating. People who ruminate cannot escape their negative and critical thoughts. They revisit past wounds and over-process past offenses repeatedly. "How could this have happened? How could he/she/they have done this to me? How can I ever forgive this? How will I ever go on? How will I ever be happy again? How much more of this do I have to take?"

If we lived in the magical world of Harry Potter, we could free ourselves from the ruminating trap by using a special incantation called "the patronus" charm. When Harry was being chased by "dementors," evil soulless creatures which plunged their victims into inescapable downward spirals of depression and despair, one of his teachers taught him this charm. He said "The Patronus is a kind of positive force, a projection of the very things that the dementor feeds upon– hope, happiness, the desire to survive– but it cannot feel despair, as real humans can, so the dementors can't hurt it."[69]

The way to conjure a patronus is to concentrate on a single happy memory and then say "*Expecto patronum*." When Harry did this, he could conjure a magical stag which chased all the dementors away.

---

[69] Rowling, J.K., Harry Potter and the Prisoner of Azkaban (New York: Arthur A. Levine Books, 1999) 237.

In the real world, there is no patronus charm, of course. But the biblical practice of lamenting serves almost the same purpose, by invoking the power of God to chase our dementors away. Lamenting is not just complaining, although it includes a time of complaining. It relies on good memories, but allows for bad ones as well. Psalm 22, one of the many laments in the *Book of Psalms* shows us how it is done. You start with all your negative feelings and memories, all your complaints. Go for full catharsis– don't hold anything back. If you are angry, you can rage at God. If you feel abandoned, say so. If you're so depressed you don't know how to move forward, say that too. Whatever is on your broken record of pain and sorrow, pour it out in its most unvarnished form: "My God, my God, why have you forsaken me? Why are you so far from helping me, from the words of my groaning...? I am a worm... scorned by others, despised by people..." But after all the darkness and pain has been spoken, the prayer is not yet over. The next step is to say something positive about God. If you cannot think of any positive memories of God in your life upon which to draw for this part, you draw instead on the memories of our ancestors as the Psalmist did. "Yet you are holy, enthroned on the praises of Israel. In you our ancestors trusted, they trusted, and you delivered them."

There are no rules about how many lines you must have in each section when you lament. The 22nd Psalm goes back and forth between complaining and proclaiming the Lord's faithfulness for several sections. It doesn't matter if you have equal parts woe and affirmation either. Most laments contain more "woe is me!" than they do "praise the Lord" in them. But they all include in them somewhere affirmations of faith. They all also include petitions to God for help. In the case of the 22nd Psalm, it is the simple statement, "Do not be far from me, for trouble is near, and there is no one to help." Now let me be clear here. The formula is not magic. Simply saying or writing a single lament won't snap you out of a lifetime of ruminating. But making lamenting a regular part of your spiritual life instead of just complaining can be transforming, and can even chase away the darkest of despair. Here's why: when we lament, we are forced to stop looking inward, and must start looking outward instead. We are forced to move from obsessing about the broken pieces of our lives to opening ourselves to the one God who has the power to birth wonderful new opportunities out of any kind of rubble. We are forced to stop thinking about our plans and what we want, and start thinking about God's plans and what God wants for us, which we know through Christ, is going to be better than anything we could dream up ourselves. We are reminded that because of the love of God, we always have reason to hope.

The spiritual practice of lamenting is grounded in the Gospel truth that there is no pain too great, no betrayal too vicious to be transformed and redeemed through the grace of God. Ann Weems, a deeply faithful Christian theologian and gifted poet, learned this lesson the hard way. On August 14, 1982, her 21-year-old son, Todd, was out celebrating his birthday. Leaving a restaurant at midnight, he noticed some men beating up a homeless man in the alley next to the restaurant. Instinctively a good Samaritan, he went to intervene. An hour later he was dead, murdered. In that moment, Weems has written, "the stars fell from my sky."[70] She was plunged into a state of such loss, despair, and anger with God and the world, that her feelings all but shut her down completely. Many of you in this congregation have experienced similar horrific losses and know all too well what I mean. When the Old Testament scholar Walter Brueggemann checked in with her repeatedly, she could not and would not be comforted. Finally, he suggested that she try to write some psalms of lament. The poet in her somehow rose to the occasion and she started to write. The results of her efforts are a book called Psalms of Lament, which I think everyone should own because it is so powerful and healing.[71] Lamenting enabled Weems to live again, moment by moment, step by step. It enabled her to find hope during her profound sorrow. It enabled her to reconnect with the God who had not abandoned her, but was weeping along with her. Now her words of pain and anguish have helped millions work through their own grief and depression, serving as prayers for all who aren't good with words themselves, or who are simply too overwhelmed to be able to speak them.

As a spiritual discipline, lamenting is an effective method for achieving personal rescue and spiritual restoration. But that is not its only

---

[70] Weems, Ann, Psalms of Lament (Louisville: Westminster John Knox Press, 1995), xv.
[71] *Ibid.*

purpose in the Old Testament. As a spiritual practice, it also served a prophetic role by leading the people of Israel to a place of communal restoration. We see this form at work in the text from the *Book of Lamentations*. Tradition says Jeremiah wrote it after the Jews were sent into Babylonian exile. Scholars now believe that is unlikely. But whoever wrote it, the point of the prolonged lament was to enable the devastated people of Israel to work through their grief to be ready for God to do something new for and with them. They were utterly paralyzed by loss. They needed to mourn the shattered pieces of their lives. They needed to cry out in pain and complaint. But they also needed to remember they were God's covenant children and therefore had reason to hope. The author of *Lamentations* gave them that reminder in one of the most painful and poignant laments recorded in history.

We don't read it much in the Christian church. I think because people believe it is depressing. There is only a single lesson from *Lamentations* included in the three-year Lectionary for use during the darkness of Holy Week. But during the raw pain poured out in these chapters, there are real words of hope we still need to hear. "The steadfast love of the Lord never ceases, his mercies never come to an end; they are new every morning; great is your faithfulness. 'The Lord is my portion,' says my soul, 'therefore I will hope in him.'" (Lam. 3:22-24). In Hebrew, *Lamentations* is called the *"Book of How."* [72] It includes all the ruminating "how could yous" and "how will I evers" that humanity has ever wanted to express. But in the professions of faith, trust and hope woven into the laments, the book also shows us "how to" open ourselves to the resurrecting newness God offers us always.

Lamenting always implicitly affirms God's resurrecting power, which may be why Jesus quoted Psalm 22 from the cross. Tradition has long held that Jesus' cries came from the depths of his humanity, which was experiencing the most extreme pain and isolation a human can feel. He needed to experience the worst of human darkness to be able to share all human experience can offer. But the fact that he quoted

---

[72] The Hebrew names of all the books in the Old Testament come from the initial verses of each book. In the case of *Lamentations*, the Hebrew word *'ekah* ("How!') comes from verses 1.1, 2.1 and 4.1.

the 22nd Psalm has led some modern commentaries to conclude that it is also possible that Jesus, in his divine wisdom, may also have chosen these words to teach his disciples one final lesson: that lamenting always leads to God and rebirth.[73] "Something more is coming," he said implicitly from the cross. "Something new is coming. Trust in God. Don't give up now. Don't get stuck in your pain. Cry out in the darkness; weep for me if you must. But then wait and watch for God's new thing because it is most assuredly coming. God has not and will never abandon you."

It is the Church's job now to share this message with our broken world. Society has the complaining part down pat. We are quick to name all the things that don't work, quick to blame and condemn our enemies, quick to mourn the loss of how things used to be, as well as the dreams we had for the future. But someone needs to show society how to move from the complaining part to the God part, from the darkness into hope. Neither political party offers this. They both play on our fears and wounds, they both at best offer only contingent hope. "We know how to save the world. Vote for us or else the nation will go to hell in a handbasket." But the hope Jesus offered from the cross, the hope that the prophets offered the exiled people of Israel is not contingent. In Christ, it is a given. It is already done. It is a gift. How might we as Christians model that kind of hope to our hurting and troubled world? I'm not sure. It's complicated of course. But I know that we've got to start by believing it ourselves. If we regularly practice the art of lamenting, turning to God even when it feels like God isn't doing enough, and holding tight to our ancestor's good memories of God's faithfulness and steadfast love, we will start to live as those who are not only open to the new beginnings God always offers, but also expect them and are looking for them. People are bound to notice the change in us; everyone is looking for reasons to hope after all.

In most of the very old copies of the 22nd Psalm, there is a cryptic subtitle under the psalm number. In the NRSV, it reads "To the leader:

---

[73] See e.g. Feasting on the Word Year B., Vol. 4, David L. Bartlett and Barbara Brown Taylor Eds. (Louisville: Westminster John Knox Press, 2009), 152-57.

according to the Deer of the Dawn, A Psalm of David." Some scholars have assumed that since the *Book of Psalms* is basically an ancient hymnal, this subtitle must refer to the name of the tune which was supposed to accompany this song of lament. Others have wondered if perhaps this was just an ancient translation error. In Hebrew, the word for help and the word for deer look very similar. Perhaps this was a lament about receiving help at dawn? But I personally like the explanation Jewish Midrash offers. According to an ancient Jewish legend, David wrote this psalm remembering his early days as a shepherd. When he was out with the sheep, his life was threatened by wild oxen, so God sent a lion to scare away the oxen. Then the lion turned on David, so God sent a deer to distract the lion.[74] Thus, verse 21 proclaims "Save me from the mouth of the lion! From the horns of the wild oxen you have rescued me." The deer of the dawn, according to the legend, is not a tune, but a tribute, not a typo, but a metaphor. God will always provide us a sacrificial deer. God already has in Christ.

Maybe J.K. Rowling had this in mind when she made up her charm. I don't know. But I do know that when we live "according to the deer of the dawn," we live as those who know that we can cry out in anger and pain and despair and God will not strike us down or condemn us. We live as those who know there is always reason to hope when we focus on God's way in Jesus Christ and not just our own. But don't just take my word for it. Listen to the words of Ann Weems, who knew far better than I that even a despairing cry from the cross can lead to a deer in the dawn. She wrote:

In the godforsaken, obscene quicksand of life,
there is a deafening alleluia
rising from the souls
of those who weep,
and of those who weep with those who weep.
If you watch, you will see
the hand of God
putting the stars back in their skies

---

[74] DeClaiseé-Walford, Nancy L., Introduction to the Psalms: A Song from Ancient Israel (St. Louis: Chalice Press, 2004), 38, (citing *Midrash Tehellim*). The legend says something "deer-like" was sent. Some say it was a gazelle, others a doe.

one by one.[75]
Amen.

---
[75] Psalms of Lament, xvii.

Divine Metrics
Ezekiel 17:22-24; Matthew 13:31-35; 44-46

In another context, the question might have been nothing more than a colorful rhetorical aside designed to make a point ("That's like asking a blind man what plaid looks like!"). But in the context of my middle school art class, my teacher's question was a sincere inquiry: "How do you explain plaid to someone born blind?" she asked. We were in the middle of exploring the color palette, mixing various colors together to make new ones. She explained that a family friend of hers had a blind daughter, who had asked her this question one day expecting that she could answer the question easily since she was an art teacher. But as we students discussed the problem in class, we quickly realized that simply saying "plaid looks like a patterned mix of three colors, such as red, green and blue," would be useless to a person who had never seen color. We had to find a way to describe plaid which did not depend upon any understanding of color, some analogy, metaphor or simile which would convey the concept and be within the girl's ability to experience. My teacher let us spend the rest of the class brainstorming, before she finally told us the way she did it.

I was reminded of that day when I first read today's Lectionary text from *Matthew*. How do you explain something like the Kingdom of Heaven to an earthbound people generally blind to the color spectrum of the divine? If you are Jesus, the answer is you use parables. Take things and experiences within the people's understanding, and then put them together in stories in such unexpected ways that the people are forced to see differently. Jesus used parables to describe all kinds of theological concepts over the course of his ministry. In today's lesson, in order to make a more powerful point, Matthew packaged together several of those parables, which the other gospels record separately, all of which describe the Kingdom of God. The text says "Kingdom of Heaven" but scholars agree that neither Matthew nor Jesus intended to refer in these texts to the place where we go after we die. The parables are all about the realm of God here and now on earth, the Kingdom which Jesus said was at hand, and nearby, within and yet to come. Matthew simply chose to follow the Jewish custom of trying to avoid using the name of God whenever possible, by substituting "heaven" for God. Jesus spoke about the Kingdom of God more than anything else in his ministry because he wanted his disciples to live in this Kingdom now, not just in heaven. He compared the Kingdom to all kinds of things within the people's experience, including in today's lesson, to a mustard seed sown in a field, yeast used by a woman making bread, a worker finding treasure in a field, and a pearl merchant finding a pearl of great value.

For most modern Christians, these parables usually evoke feelings of pleasure. We like the image of the mustard tree with birds sheltered in its branches, and of bread rising and baking -- what's not to like about that? Every real estate agent will tell you that you can increase the possibility of selling your house if it is filled with that wonderful yeasty smell of homemade bread cooking. We love treasure too, of course, whether it comes from unexpectedly discovering the winning lottery ticket blowing across a parking lot, or from being an astute enough entrepreneur to recognize a golden investment before it skyrockets in value. But for Jesus' First Century hearers, these parables were shockingly subversive, so much so that many scholars consider the lessons conveyed in this collection of little Kingdom sayings to be among the most radical of Jesus' teachings. They are still radical today, if we understand and take seriously what they affirm. So, I want to spend some time this morning exploring why.

In the first story, someone takes mustard seed and sows it into a field where it grows until it becomes, according to *Matthew's* version of this story, a tree in which the birds come to nest. That all sounds good until we realize that no Jewish farmer in his right mind would ever sow mustard in a field. To do so would be in some ways the equivalent of planting a nice little batch of kudzu or Virginia creeper in the middle of your crop. In the Holy Land, mustard is not a rare specimen plant, it is a hugely common, invasive, crop-destroying, uncontrollable weed. Furthermore, any First Century Jew who planted mustard in another crop would not only violate the laws of common sense, he would also violate the purity and holiness laws set forth in *Leviticus* which prohibited mixing seeds in fields. (See e.g. Lev. 19:19). Thus, for folk hearing this story for the first time, it would have sounded like Jesus was saying something like "the Kingdom of God is like an uncontrollable corrupting influence."

For the educated Pharisees and scribes and Sadducees in Jesus' audience, his message would have sounded even worse because of the tree imagery he chose to use. The language of a great tree which shelters all the birds and animals was very well known to them. In Mesopotamian culture, the image was a classic, triumphant image of empire known as the "cosmic" tree. In Jewish tradition, that image was used by the prophets to describe the day when the kingdom of Israel would triumph over all the nations. As we heard from *Ezekiel* this morning, the people of Israel were supposed to become like a great and noble cedar on a mountain top after their exile. They were to become like a supernatural cedar which not only sheltered all the birds, but also somehow produced abundant fruit. This was how the Kingdom of God was supposed to look: triumphant, majestic, and bigger than everything else. Not like shrubbery! Matthew may have generously called the mustard a tree, but the other gospel writers were more honest. Mustard is a shrub; at best, it gets to be 6-8 feet tall. Even being the "greatest of all shrubs" sounds pretty lame compared to a cedar on a mountain top. Was Jesus saying the Kingdom of God was both corrupting and unimpressive?

While they were trying to figure this out, Jesus' next parable would have convinced them that he was crazy or evil or both. "The Kingdom of God is like a woman who puts yeast in three measures of flour until it is all leavened" Jesus said. In Jewish culture, yeast was another symbol of corruption and it frequently served as a metaphor for the human sin of pride. Thus, the Talmud records Rabbi Alexandri ending all his prayers with the phrase, "Sovereign of the Universe, it is full known well to Thee that our will is to perform Thy will, and what prevents us? The yeast in the dough..."[76] All bread offerings to God had to be unleavened according to *Leviticus,* and all yeast eradicated from the home before Passover. (See e.g. Lev. 2:11, 6:17). Unleavened bread was holy; leavened bread was corrupt. This is because yeast in Jesus day did not come from a nice little Fleischmann's package, it came from exposing flour and water to wild yeast until they fermented naturally into a kind of sourdough starter. Leaven, in other words, was sour, spoiled flour. In the parable,

---

[76] As quoted in *Robinson, Rich, "Lessons from Leaven,"* in *Jews for Jesus Newsletter, Mar.* 2, 2007 (citing the Babylonian Talmud, Berakoth 17a, Soncino Ed., 100), retrieved from http://jewishroots.net/library/holiday-articles/lessons_from_leaven.html

the woman leavened or corrupted three full measures of flour, which would have made enough bread to feed 150 people, not just herself. What was Jesus thinking celebrating a kingdom that was corrupting, unimpressive and wasteful? And how could he then turn around and imply through the next two parables that this weed-invested, wasteful kingdom was so valuable that whether it was discovered accidentally or intentionally, it was worth people selling all their belongings to gain? Pearls in Jesus' day, in both Roman and Jewish culture were considered symbols of the highest possible good. "Was the kingdom good or bad, holy or unholy, desirable or undesirable?" the Jews who heard Jesus must have wondered after hearing these descriptions. What he said just didn't seem to make practical or spiritual sense.

We may enjoy mustard and leavened bread now, but that does not mean that Jesus' images of the Kingdom make more sense to us now theologically than they did to Jews in his day. In fact, if we take them at all seriously, they should shake us up just as much and as quickly because we, like his first listeners, like to assume that our standards and God's standards are one and the same; these parables reveal that that is simply not the case. For us the measures of success and the benchmarks of empire are size and wealth and power. We are driven by a love of metrics: How much did profits increase in the past quarter? What is the size of the corporation, the constituency, the membership? Whose military is bigger and more powerful? Whose portfolio more impressive? In America, especially, even greatness isn't good enough. We are a people who seek to be exceptional. We want to be the cedar on the mountain top. But Jesus' images turn all our metrics on their heads. In these parables about the Kingdom success is not measured by size or speed, efficiency or purity, material wealth, corporate profitability, fame or even familiarity.

Here then is why scholars consider these parables so subversive both for First Century Jews and 21st Century Christians. Instead of describing the Kingdom of God in terms that we would expect and desire– for the ancient Jews in terms of law and purity and triumphant empire– and for us in terms of size and power, economics and status, Jesus describes the Kingdom in almost exactly opposite terms. He celebrates weeds and yeast, unpredictable growth beyond our control and success without status. He emphasizes hiddenness over high visibility and humility over fame. In so doing, he basically gives us a choice. If we want to dwell in the kingdom here and now, we must reorder our value system. If we are unwilling to do this, and prefer to hold onto our world's value system, then we must find a way to dismiss what Jesus said in some way. In Jesus' day, people did this by arguing that Jesus was advocating corruption. In our day, Christians do this by making these texts about themselves instead of God, arguing they are about personal salvation – being clever enough to be counted among those who have found the hidden treasure or pearl, or about the inevitability of church growth. We redefine the Kingdom of God according to our world's metrics, instead of the other way around.

But it's never too late for us to change that. We can embrace God's metrics over our world's if we keep in mind two things. First, as Warren Carter put it, "if a person is well adjusted to a sick society, corrupting is the only path to wholeness."[77] In other words, Jesus was not offering these parables to deprive us of enjoying a healthy world. He was offering these parables to show us the way to an experience of wholeness and joy that our world cannot give. The more that his values sound counter-cultural, crazy, irrelevant or unfamiliar, therefore, the more they should warn us that our world has gone very, very wrong since God first created it. However well-adjusted we are to its values, it is we who are now off track, not Jesus. When we understand this, then continuing to cling to our world's ways makes less and less sense.

The second thing for us to keep in mind is that Jesus did not offer the images of the Kingdom he did just to reject the values of the world. He also was trying to explain to a spiritually blind people how to recognize the Kingdom he came to proclaim was at hand. He did this by offering images which are not just subversive, they are also sublime and suggestive, if we consider them through the lens of God's grace and love.

Consider for example, that mustard in the field again. It turns out that what the mustard plant lacks in size, it makes up for in medicinal power. According to First Century Roman historian Pliny, mustard in

---

[77] As quoted in <u>Feasting on the Word,</u> Year A., Vol. 3, David L. Bartlett and Barbara Brown Taylor, Eds. (Louisville: Westminster John Knox Press, 2011), 286.

Jesus' day was used to treat serpent bites and scorpion stings. It counteracted the poison in fungi, treated sinus trouble, tooth aches, stomach troubles, bowel impaction and bladder problems.[78] In our day, mustard is used to cure sore throats and congested chests, to enhance beauty, remove noxious smells and more. It was the main ingredient in the first cancer drug ever developed, and is still used to battle leukemia.[79] Jesus was not just talking about shrubbery toppling mighty trees, he was also painting a picture of our divinely-given means of wholeness. "The Kingdom of God is like someone who plants seeds of healing," he effectively said, "which render the poisons of the world impotent and heal human brokenness. These seeds grow and grow and cannot be stopped. They will keep popping up until healing is ubiquitous and available to all of God's creatures." Imagine what our world would look like if we valued healing, long term growth and reconciliation more than size, speed and power. Can you glimpse the golden flowers of the kingdom popping up around you?

While you are imagining that, consider that mad bread-baking woman again as well. By using yeast, she took something invisibly small, and grew it into a veritable feast able to feed at least 150 people. She took something that was considered spoiled, and used it to make something sustaining for a whole community. We all know how much Jesus liked to describe God in terms of a heavenly feast. Here is that feast, from the perspective of the back kitchen. The Kingdom of God is a realm characterized by extravagant generosity and unexpected hospitality. The Kingdom of God is a realm in which there was enough grace for everyone to be fed and welcomed to the table. The Kingdom of God is a realm in which nothing and no one is too small, too spoiled or too sinful to be transformed by

---

[78] Pliny, Natural History, 20.87.236-237, as cited in, Prophetic Witness: An Appropriate Contemporary Mode of Public Discourse? Heinrich Bedford-Strohm and Etienne de Villiers Eds. (Zurich: LIT VERLAG GmbH & Co., 2011), 56.

[79] The original source for this, "Mustard" listing, INNVISTA, at http://www.innvista.com/healthy/herbs/mustard.htm is no longer available at this link. For comparable information, *see* Smith, Andrew D., "*From Warfare to Mainstay: Mustard Derivatives Play Evolving Role in Cancer Therapy*", ONC LIVE, posted Jan. 19, 2012, retrievable at http://www.onclive.com/publications/oncology-live/2011/november-2011/from-warfare-to-mainstay-mustard-derivatives-play-evolving-role-in-cancer-therapy#sthash.ylYurjLe.dpuf

God's love. Do you think we would be decrying the wastefulness of it all if we could dine regularly at that kind of feast? Imagine if everyone in our world ascribed the highest value to the traits of generosity and hospitality, and gave the highest priority to magnifying God's grace for the good of the community not just the individual? Can you catch a whiff of that heavenly smell coming from the back kitchen?

My art teacher decided to describe plaid to the blind girl using modeling clay. She made three distinct strips of clay by varying their width, texture and roundness. Then she wove them together in a classic plaid pattern. It wasn't the same as the girl's being able to see the colors, but it was better than just words. After that, although she could not see plaid, she knew what it felt like, and could image what it would look like in her mind's eye. Is the Kingdom of God so different? Thomas Merton once said, "Life is this simple. We are living in a world that is transparent, and God is shining through it all the time. This is not just a fable or nice story. It is true.... The only thing is that we don't see it."[80] Maybe we don't always see the Kingdom that Jesus proclaimed again and again was already at hand. But through his parables he has enabled us to know what it feels like. It is a realm of healing and wholeness, generosity and hospitality, grace and love, where status and wealth and power are irrelevant, and diversity and community trump purity and individualism. It is a Kingdom which makes so much sense and offers so much security that whether you stumble across it accidentally, or find it after years of seeking, it will change what you value forever. It's already here, although not yet fully realized. Step into the realm of God's metrics, embrace them as your own, and watch the Kingdom grow. Amen.

---

[80] *"Thomas Merton Quotes"* entry, Thinkexist.com, retrieved at http://thinkexist.com/quotation/life-is-this-simple-we-are-living-in-a-world-that/557804.html

Gates of Meeting
1 Kings 17:8-24; Luke 7:11-17

Last Sunday I began a Lenten sermon series on passages in the Bible which mention gates or doors, as a means of helping us consider the spiritual and emotional gates and doors that we encounter in our own lives and journeys of faith. We considered what it means that Jesus said that he was the "door of the sheep," and found that it meant, among other things, that Jesus was the prophesied "door of hope" God promised to lead us out of valleys of trouble. But knowing there is always a door which leads out of darkness and into God's presence is not the same thing as knowing where to find that doorknob in the darkness. So today, we are going to consider what the stories of two famous widows who were shown doors of hope by God, can teach us about where to look for our own.

There are many similarities between the stories of how the great prophet, Elijah the Tishbite, led the widow of Zarephath into hope, and how Jesus led the widow of Nain there. Luke wanted to make the parallels between the two miraculous incidents obvious in order to show that Jesus was greater and more powerful than even the greatest of prophets. So, although Elijah's story alone includes a food miracle, both stories involve widows losing their only sons, and both include those sons being brought back to life by God. But for purposes of our Lenten journey, a far less dramatic similarity interests me the most. Both stories begin outside the gates of cities.

This similarity in setting is not significant historically because almost everything took place outside city gates in Jesus' day, and centuries earlier in Elijah's day as well. If you walked to the gates, at any given time, you might hear someone making announcements about the laws, or events in the city; you might also see a judicial case being tried, see people selling and buying various wares, slaves, (or themselves), see a wedding party, or a funeral procession or a capital sentencing. If you can imagine what it would be like to combine the activities and purposes of our modern airports, malls, capital buildings, court houses, and red light districts, with the kind of military presence we see at the gates at Ft. Meade or the Naval Academy, then you begin to get the idea. It was at a city gate that

Tamar could trick Judah into doing right by her, and at a city gate that Boaz was given the right to become the husband of Ruth. The Bible is filled with city gate stories in part because of the architecture and culture of the region. But it is also filled with them in part because from a theological perspective, city gates were symbolically significant. As Grayde Parsons has observed, they are theologically-loaded locations by virtue of the fact that they were "the great equalizers."[81] The city gate was one of the few locations where you could find rich and poor, healthy and sick, young and old, powerful and powerless, Jew and Gentile, happy and sad at the same time. That is important to keep in mind as we look at today's miracle stories.

The reason that Elijah showed up at the gate of Zarephath, a city in the foreign territory of Sidon, not in Israel, is that he was hiding. Angered by the evil doing of the king and queen of Israel, Ahab and Jezebel, Elijah had told them that God would punish them with a three-year drought. They did not appreciate this news. So, God sent Elijah to Sidon, to escape both them and the drought. At first God took care of Elijah by sending him to live by a stream where ravens fed him. But when our story begins, the stream has dried up and God has ordered Elijah to go into town. Elijah needed people, and as it turns out, the person he encountered, needed him.

The widow of Zarephath had nothing. Apparently, her deceased husband did not leave her with a brother or father-in-law to take care of her. In Jewish tradition, the laws of Levirate marriage required the nearest male relative to marry the widow, in part to protect her. But this woman was not a Jew, so she had little or no means of providing for herself, and was gathering sticks for a fire which would help her cook her last meal, before she and her son would starve to death. Elijah first opened the door to hope and new life for her by demanding that she give him a drink and then cook for him. His tone sounds more bossy and entitled than compassionate at first, which always bothers me when I read this passage. But there was method to his madness. God had promised to provide for Elijah's need while he

---

[81] Parsons, Grayde, <u>Open to Me the Gates</u> (Louisville: Witherspoon Press, 2012), 3.

was in hiding. So, as long as the widow was providing for him, Elijah knew that God would ensure she had enough for herself too.

The miracle of the grain and oil was not enough to save her son, however. Without him, the widow was more than grief-stricken, she was in great danger. With no heir and no male in her life, she would lose what little she had left. So, Elijah intervened again. Praying to God on the widow's behalf, not the boy's, Elijah could bring the boy back to life, and in so doing, reveal to the widow the way out of the valley of the shadow of death.

The widow of Nain in the New Testament lesson is given this same door, when Jesus revives her son. This time the encounter takes place after the son is dead however. Jesus and his disciples and followers are heading into Nain through the gate while the widow is heading with mourners outside the gate to bury her son. Moved by her tears, Jesus revives the son with remarkably little fanfare. He does not ask her about her faith. He does not share a meal with her. No one even offers a fervent prayer to God. Jesus has the power on his own to do what Elijah did with God's help. He just brings the boy back and continues his way. But as was the case when Elijah worked his miracle, Jesus' revival of the son is a double revival. In that moment, he saves the widow from a very dark valley of trouble, and a strong potential for death. Although he renders himself ritually unclean by touching the body, Jesus does the opposite for the widow. He brings her out of an isolation caused by death, back into community, out of danger and back into safety.

These stories, as well as the many others which record events of great theological significance taking place at gates suggest that gates in the bible stand symbolically for two theological truths. The first is that God likes to hang out at city gates. It is the place where God heals and liberates. God likes places where people who might not otherwise ever meet are thrown together. These places are "thin spots" which give us a fleeting glimpse of the kingdom of God, where people will come from north, south, east and west.

The second theological truth we learn at the gates is that the way God likes to lead people out of the valley of trouble and into new life is by moving them from isolation back into community. This certainly was the case with the widow of Nain's miracle, and with the widow of Zarephath. Their isolation was potentially destructive; they needed others to be safe and whole again. But in the Old Testament story, even the miracle worker Elijah is healed in this way too. Jewish Midrash says that Elijah was known for disliking having to rely on other people.[82] But in this story, he needed to come out of hiding and to rely on another to survive. The stream that had been his salvation had dried up. He needed water, and food. The widow, with God's help, gave him both.

The theological phrase used to describe the way that God saves people in these stories by connecting them to others is called, "the soteriology of with-ness."[83] That is a mouthful! But all it means is that God offers the people salvation by being with them in and through others. God meets them at the gates in unexpected ways and people, recognizes their suffering, and then connects them with others in such a way that they are saved. The primary way that *Luke* illustrates how God saved humanity through Christ is with "withness." "Today you will be *with me* in Paradise" Jesus says to the criminal, while the two of them hang on crosses just outside the city gates. This story and all the many healing stories and parables before it in *Luke* tell us that if you want to find God, if you want to find a doorway to hope, the best place to look is to look at a gate.

But what is the modern American equivalent of a biblical city gate? We don't live in walled cities anymore; and I don't think anyone here would argue that a surefire way to encounter God is to hang out near Route 3 at the Crofton gate. No, I think if we want to find today's gates, we must think much less literally. What makes the gates special in the Bible is not their architectural structure, but their function. They are places that bring together people who otherwise wouldn't be together. When we had the big snow storm a few weeks ago, for example, you may have stumbled upon a city gate right in the middle of your unplowed street. I know I did. I went outside and soon discovered that the snow had magically turned a bunch of strangers into a community. My next-door neighbor, whose last name I don't

---

[82] See Kadari, Tamar. "*Widow of Zarephath: Midrash and Aggadah*," Jewish Women: A Comprehensive Historical Encyclopedia. 1 March 2009. Jewish Women's Archive. (Viewed on Feb. 17, 2016)
<http://jwa.org/encyclopedia/article/widow-of-zarephath-midrash-andaggadah>

[83] See Karris, Robert J., "*Luke's Soteriology of 'With-ness'*," CURRENTS IN THEOLOGY AND MISSION, 12 No. 6, Dec. 1985, 346-352.

even know, came over unasked to help shovel my sidewalks. People across the street were chatting and offering to share snow blowers. In that moment (or for that long and painful week depending on how you look at it), we all were trapped together, and so found ourselves living together, instead of just next to each other. We shared food and laughter and complaints about sore backs, and in so doing, moved from being isolated by the snow, to being drawn into community because of it.

You have probably experienced other city gate moments like this. Maybe you found yourself making new friends at an airport when your flight was delayed and you had to sleep with 40 strangers on the floor around gate 27. Maybe you experienced a city gate moment serving dinner at a shelter like Sarah's House, or laying flooring at a Habitat house. Maybe you discovered a gate in your own living room when you got sick or injured yourself and were forced, against your will, to rely on the kindness and help of others for a time. In these moments when we find ourselves sharing space and time with others, either because of circumstances or by choice, we can rest assured that God is with us. God loves hanging out at the gates, so you never know what will happen.

But there is another city gate which is more permanent than the kind that is created by a snow storm, and that is the Church. Some of us here are actual neighbors. But most of us would not cross paths much in our daily lives if it were not for this church. Yet Christ has called us here, young and old, married and single, grieving and rejoicing together so that instead of being isolated by our faith, we can have community to strengthen and support us. God created the Church universal so that humankind would be able to have a door of hope in the same way that the widows did, by making a place where Christ likes to hang out, and where we can help each other move out of dangerous isolation. As the poet Rumi writes: "Where Jesus lives, the great-hearted gather. We are a door that's never locked. If you are suffering any kind of pain, stay near this door. Open it."[84]

In our age of "bowling alone" there are not many places that can offer the saving ""with-ness" of God that the Church can, even

---

[84] The Essential Rumi, Coleman Barks Trans. (San Francisco: HarperCollins, 2004), 201.

with all its flaws. You can go to the gym and find people of all ages, but it is rare to find there the kind of friends that would drop everything to sit and weep with you. You can join a club or go to work and find people who share your interests, but you may not find people in those places whose interests are the opposite of yours in exactly the way you need. The Church is different. God has made this community more than we ourselves. God has called us together to be with us and lead us into new life. Were it not for God, some of us would live lives of isolation. Were it not for God, some of us would have great needs and no way of finding help. But because we have come together, we now have others who can help us and we can be the help ourselves.

Author Kathleen Norris puts it this way, "In the rural area where I live, churches are still the only institutions capable of sustaining community ministries such as a food pantry and a domestic violence hot line. But they provide something more that even the most well-intentioned Asocial services" cannot replace. It is called salvation but it begins small, at the local level, in a church that provides a time and place for people to gather to meet a God who has promised to be here. People are encouraged to sing, whether they can or not. And they receive a blessing, just for showing up."[85] In *Proverbs* Chapter 8, the Holy Spirit, who is called Lady Wisdom, cries out to all from the gates in front of town, "at the entrance of the portals she cries out: "To you, O people, I call and my cry is to all that live.... I have good advice and sound wisdom; I have insight, I have strength.... I love those who love me, and those who seek me diligently find me.... Happy is the one who listens to me, watching daily at my gates, waiting beside my doors. For whoever finds me finds life and obtains favor from the Lord; but those who miss me injure themselves; all who hate me love death." (Prov. 8:3-4, 14, 17, 34-36). Look for the gates as they present themselves throughout your day. And look for the proverbial widows here, who like you gather at this gate to find the help they need. Christ is there and here. He who brings strangers together is our source of life and strength. Thanks be to God! Amen.

---

[85] Norris, Kathleen, Amazing Grace: A Vocabulary of Faith (New York: Riverhead Books, 1998), 261.

God in the Here and Now

Maternal Blessings
Isaiah 49: 1, 14-16; Matthew 23:37-39

In 2007, William Paul Young wrote a work of fiction about how a father whose daughter was kidnapped and murdered could work through his profound grief and anger thanks to a miraculous weekend encounter with God. His book, The Shack,[86] became an instant *New York Times* bestseller. It's not surprising such a book would interest people; after all, the problem of human suffering for those who believe in an all-powerful and loving God, a problem known as theodicy, has been a compelling one for Christians for millennia. But in the case of The Shack, it wasn't the special wisdom of Young's views about theodicy that most often made people pick up the book; it was the controversy surrounding his portrayal of the Godhead. Young shocked a lot of people by depicting God, the Father, as an African American grandmother, living in divine relationship with Jesus and with the Holy Spirit, who appeared as a constantly moving, slightly transparent Asian woman.

Young's work was fiction of course, so whether most Christians approve of his theology does not matter as far as the future of the Church is concerned. But the fact that so many Christians were made uncomfortable by the thought of God being depicted in strong maternal terms is a problem because it shows what a poor job the Church has done lately to educate believers about the fullness of the Triune God whom we love and serve. Christian doctrine has always affirmed that God embodies both male and female qualities, as well as divine characteristics like omnipotence and omniscience, which are utterly beyond the realm of human experience and even understanding. *Genesis* confirms that God is beyond our traditional human understanding of gender in its proclamation that *both* man and woman were made in God's image and likeness. (Gen. 1:27).

One of the reasons that Christians get confused about the Trinity and gender is that Jesus of Nazareth was a human male. Another

---

[86] Young, Wm. Paul, The Shack: Where Tragedy Confronts Eternity, (Newbury Park, Windblown Media, 2007).

reason is that the Church has always referred to God as Jesus did, as Father. Hearing the word "Father" repeatedly can prompt one's unconscious to generate male mental images of God. But what we have lost through the ages is the appreciation that since Jesus' day, orthodox Christianity has always affirmed that our use of the name "Father" for God has nothing to do with gender. It has always been a term to describe the nature of our intimate relationship with God, not God's maleness. Thus, in the 2nd Century, Christian theologian Clement of Alexandria, who called God "Father," also freely celebrated what he identified as the maternal love of God evidenced by the Incarnation.[87] Going one step further, in the 4th Century, Archbishop of Constantinople, Gregory of Nazianzus, expressly criticized all who incorrectly assumed that God was male because of the use of the name "Father," while Bishop Augustine of Hippo celebrated God as both father and mother of us all in his writing. Still later, even after the Church had become more patriarchal in the Middle Ages, the language people used for the Godhead was much more inclusive than it is today. For example, in the 11th Century, Anselm of Canterbury, one of the most influential theologians in Christian history prayed, "But you too, good Jesus, are you not also a mother?... Christ, my mother, you gather your chickens under your wings; this dead chicken of yours puts himself under those wings.... Warm your chicken, give life to your dead one, justify your sinner."[88]

Christian artwork has also celebrated God in male and female terms. The Church of Dominus Flevit, which overlooks Jerusalem from the Mount of Olives, chose as its central symbol of the gospel behind the communion table a mosaic depicting God-as-mother-hen text from today's gospel lesson, which also served as inspiration for Anselm's Prayer.[89]

---

[87] All the references to Church history theologians in this paragraph come from Johnson, Elizabeth, "*The Incomprehensibility of God and the Image of God Male and Female,*" THEOLOGICAL STUDIES, vol. 45, no.3, 1984, 441-465, retrieved from www.womanpriests.org/classic/johnson3.asp

[88] As quoted in Johnson, Elizabeth A., She Who Is: The Mystery of God in Feminist Theological Discourse, (New York: Crossroad Pub. Co, 1997), 150.

[89] Mosaic in Dominus Flevit Church, Mount of Olives, Jerusalem, Israel; picture by Anton 17 - Own work, CC BY-SA 3.0, https://commons.wikimedia.org/w/index.php?curid=28575619 (Used with permission.)

Similarly, this 14th Century Bavarian fresco of the Trinity found in St. James church in Urshalling, Germany, depicts Father, Son, and a female Holy Spirit all wearing the same cloak together, inspired by the long standing tradition that the Holy Spirit most embodies the "feminine" traits of the Godhead.[90]

I'm not sure exactly when speaking of God in both male and female terms stopped being perceived positively as mainstream and meaningful by all Christians. But I think that one of the reasons some

modern Christians are less comfortable with mixing up genders, names and metaphors for God than our ancestors in the faith were, is that modern Christians are far less familiar with the Bible than

---

[90] Trinity Fresco in St. James Church, Ürshalling, Germany.

previous generations of Christians used to be. So we do not realize that the Word of God itself is the Church's source for all the mixed metaphors. Thankfully, that is an easy problem to fix. And what better day to do so than today, when people across the country are celebrating the blessings mothers provide? But before I refresh our recollection of some of the biblical texts which have inspired so many Christians before us to celebrate the feminine and maternal qualities of our Triune God, I want to be clear that in doing so I am not suggesting that the Church should abandon Father language in favor of calling God exclusively Mother. Both paternal and maternal images for God are biblical and valuable. So, if you are more comfortable with Father language in your prayers that is fine with me. But I do think that it is important for us to appreciate, on this day especially, that regardless of how we refer to God, we all have been blessed by the maternal love of a God who will never forget us, or stop thinking of us as beloved children no matter what we do.

There are many texts in the Bible which use female images to characterize God's nature or God's role with humankind. God is described in the *Psalms* as a midwife (Ps. 22:9-10), and in Jesus' parables as a woman leavening bread (Luke 13:18-21) and looking for a lost coin. (Luke 15:8-10). In addition to being a mother hen who offers protection under her wings in *Matthew*, God is also a protective mother bear in *Hosea* (13:8), and a protective mother eagle in *Deuteronomy* (32:11-12), and *Exodus* (19:4). But the imagery that is perhaps the most powerful and evocative is the imagery of God not as a mother animal, but as the mother of humankind, spoken by the prophets Isaiah and Hosea. "Can a woman forget her nursing child, or show no compassion for the child of her womb?" says the Lord through Isaiah in today's Old Testament lesson. "Even these may forget you, yet I will not forget you. See I have inscribed you on the palm of my hands." "Listen to me, O house of Jacob, all the remnant of the house of Israel, you who have been borne by me from your birth, carried from the womb," God says in an earlier passage. "Even when you turn gray I will carry you. I have made and I will bear; I will carry and will save." (Is. 46:3-4; see also Deut. 32:18 for more divine birth imagery.) "As a mother comforts her child, so I will comfort you" God continues a few chapters later. (Is. 66:12 13). Hosea, who prophesied before Isaiah, paints his picture of God's mothering in terms which remind me of a mother flipping through a baby book:

"When Israel was a child I loved him and out of Egypt I called my son.... [I]t was I who taught Ephraim to walk, I took them up in my arms; but they did not know that I healed them. I led them with cords of human kindness, with bands of love. I was to them like those who lift infants to their cheeks. I bent down to them and fed them.... How can I give you up, Ephraim?... My heart recoils within me; my compassion grows warm and tender.... I am God and no mortal, the Holy One in your midst, and I will not come in wrath." (Hos. 11:1, 3-4, 8-9).

So many of the divine characteristics and traits which Christian tradition celebrates are those we typically (or stereotypically) think of as male: God as the all-powerful one; God as the Judge and Disciplinarian; God as the one who led the people into battle; God as the one who with rod and staff shepherds the sheep. Without the maternal texts to round out our impression of God, we might not fully appreciate that one of God's greatest powers is the power to nurture and comfort us in all circumstances, nor that God's judgments are biased by the kind of maternal love which comes from spending endless sleepless nights feeding, nursing, and scaring goblins away, and endless days watching for and celebrating with deep investment and joy every developmental milestone achieved. We might not think of God's commands as essential to our health and well-being as a mother's advice not to forget a jacket when it's cold, or never to run in the street, or always to share and say "please" and "thank you." We might never picture God running to get bacitracin and a Band-Aid when we fall, singing us a lullaby when we're tired, or bending down with arms wide, ready to give a hug when we're feeling unloved or scared.

This makes these metaphors very valuable. It's not that fathers can't be nurturing or mothers can't be powerful and strong. Of course, they can and they are. To equate certain traits with certain genders is inevitably to stereotype to some degree. But even though they are stereotypes, the fact is that these labels remain emotionally evocative for most of us. We think of certain images, certain experiences from our own lives when we hear the word "Father," and other images and experiences when we hear the word "Mother." Stop and think for a minute. What feelings does the word "mother" evoke in you?

Father Ray Suriani tells the story of what the word meant to some school children.[91] One day a teacher was trying to teach her 2nd grade class about how magnets work. She spent the day talking about magnetic attraction, and how magnets could be used as tools. The next day she decided to give her class a little pop quiz. One of the questions she put on the quiz was "My name has six letter. The first one is M. I pick up things. What am I?" Almost half of the class got the question wrong. They answered "mother" instead of magnet. But the response made the teacher smile so much she decided to give them credit anyway. I guess she had picked up enough of her own children's dirty laundry and toys to see that their answer was correct, if not the one she originally sought.

When we think of mothers, perhaps we, too, think of someone who picks things up and cleans up our messes. Maybe we think of someone who cooks dinner, as my four-year old son volunteered in his own class the other day when asked what mothers do. If we have been or are blessed with wonderful mothers, we may think of someone who was always there, always able to make our hurts feel better; someone who loves us no matter what and is our fiercest defender and most enthusiastic cheerleader. Imagine for a moment how our relationship with God might change if we could also think of our God this way?

I think our change in perspective might influence our discipleship in three significant ways. First, we might start thinking of God a little less like a judge to be feared, and less like a white, male, bearded Santa Claus figure who is supposed to give us stuff if we say and do certain things, and might instead start thinking about God as our source of unconditional and uncompromising love, as our "ground and power of being" as theologian Paul Tillich put it.[92] The one who made us, who has nursed us with grace and love since the moment of our birth, will fight for us and forgive us more than any other. But that

---

[91] Suriani, Fr. Ray, *"Four Things a Good Mother Never Forgets,"* a homily delivered May 9, 2010 at St. Pius X Church, Westerly, R.I, posted to *"Father Ray's Other Corner Blog,"* May 9, 2010, (12:32 p.m.),
http://fatherrays.blogspot.com/2010/05/four-things-good-mother-never-forgets.html

[92] Tillich, Paul, Systematic Theology, Vol. Two, (Chicago: Univ. Chicago Press, 1957), 10.

God also has high expectations for our behavior, and big dreams for what we can make of our lives. Therefore, we must recognize the wisdom of Christ's teachings as essential, not just for getting into heaven, but for having rich and full lives here and now. We must yearn to stay connected to our ground of being as much as a hungry infant yearns for her mother's milk. Thinking of God in maternal terms helps us to do this.

Second, if we fully appreciated the maternal qualities of our God, I think we might also be slower to condemn others in God's name than we are now. Human beings are so quick to judge one another. Our criteria for sinfulness vary– some people judge based upon appearance, others upon ideology, and still others upon behaviors. But these maternal texts remind us that God does not judge the way that we do. God sees us first and foremost as children. Yes, God sees our sins; but God also sees inside our hearts down to the people we were born to be. God knows the hurts in life that lead us into sin, and how inadequate we are most of the time to rise above them. "How can I hand you over, O Israel?" God asks in *Hosea*. "You are my baby boy! You are my baby girl!" If we better appreciated the maternal sorrow and compassion our own behavior provokes in God, maybe we would have an easier time seeing our neighbors, even our sinful neighbors, as God's children as well.

Finally, the third blessing that comes from reclaiming the maternal images of God in Scripture is that we are reminded that we all are blessed to experience a good mother's love, even if we have not been blessed in this life with a good human mother to share this with us. Mother's Day is a hard day for a lot of people. Not everyone grows up with a loving, affirming mother, or even knowing a human mother. For those people, these texts offer divine comfort to answer the pain of "if only." God even now is showering you with a mother's love. God even now is eager to listen and wipe away your tears; God is beaming with pride over your accomplishments, and wants nothing more than to hold your hand and walk with you into the future. Our divine mother hen will never forget or abandon you.

In 1988, long before The Shack was written, a Puerto Rican woman named Inez was asked by an interviewer how she envisioned God. She said, "[I]f they would ask me to draw God, I would draw my grandmother smiling. Because she is the only person that I believe has filled me or filled me so much that I can compare her with God. I would draw a picture of my grandmother with her hands open, smiling, as if to say, 'Come with me because I am waiting for you.' God is strength for the *lucha* [the struggle], strength to keep going, to encourage."[93] On this day, may we rejoice with all the saints who have gone before us in the knowledge that we have a God who, like a mother or grandmother, reaches out to us with a big smile and open arms. No matter what we have done or what is making us struggle, we have a God whose outstretched palms will be forever etched with our names. Amen

---

[93] Johnson, Elizabeth A., She Who Is, 146.

Once in Woodrow Wilson Service Station
A Christmas Eve Homily

"And all this took place to fulfill what has been spoken by the Lord through the prophet, 'Look, the virgin shall conceive and bear a son, and they shall name him Emmanuel....'" (Matt. 1:22-23). We have heard these words a million times, perhaps so many times that we don't even ponder their meaning anymore, especially on nights like tonight when everything seems cloaked in warm candlelight and wonder. So, I was a bit surprised when I heard recently that this verse was troubling someone. The person was not troubled by the idea of a virgin birth, as many people today are, nor was she worried about the fact that the prophecy Matthew references was originally delivered more than 600 years earlier to an evil Judean king to get him to trust in God. He didn't, and Judah was conquered as a consequence. No, the problem for this particular person was that Jesus was never named Emmanuel. How can Christians believe that this prophecy was fulfilled as Matthew said, the person wanted to know, when Joseph and Mary named the baby Jesus, instead of Emmanuel?

The quick answer is, of course, that this prophecy was not about the Christ child's given name, but about his role. Jesus came into the world and was Emmanuel, God-with-us, for those who followed him. He was understood to be God incarnate then, and is understood that way by Christians now. But the question got me thinking about what it means that God came into the world to be with us, not in splendor and glory, but with us in the trenches of human existence. Perhaps we have sentimentalized the stable scene too much. Perhaps we are so used to picturing doe-eyed cattle and angel-inspired shepherds, that we have forgotten that Christ's birth was scandalous in its inappropriateness given that Jesus was God's chosen King. We have mentally sanitized away the smell of manure and sour straw, and overlooked the exhaustion and fear that that poor teenage girl must have felt. We have forgotten the crowds filling every nook and cranny of Bethlehem so that their oppressor, Caesar, could tax an already poor people still more. We imagine cute children in bathrobes when we hear shepherds, instead of thinking of the baby Jesus' first visitors as shifty, dishonest and despised nomads, as the people in Jesus' day did. In other words, perhaps the problem is that the whole birth story doesn't feel as it did then, as if God was slumming it in a radical way, nor does it feel that God is truly with *us* in life as we know it now. The story feels more like God captured in a pretty, ancient Christmas card than God coming unexpectedly into the last place you would think to look for a savior or a king, just so that we would know the depths of God's love.

So tonight, I want to bring the baby into a more familiar setting. If Jesus were being born today, the birth would most likely be in third world refugee camp or an inner-city ghetto. Jesus would be born wherever life is hard for most people, where suffering is real, and where ordinary folk struggle with the elements, not mingle with the power elite. Our Lord Emmanuel came to experience everyday life during our greatest challenges and pain so that we would know that God truly understands us-- our fears and our shortcomings, our hurts and our dreams. There is no place in this world too lowly for God to dwell, no person too inconsequential or sinful to save.

But since they say you're supposed to write what you know, for tonight, instead of imagining Jesus being born in a crack house or a shack in foreign mountains somewhere, I imagined him being born a little closer to home, in a setting I know all too well thanks to years of driving to New York to visit family for the holidays. I hope as I share this story with you, you will think about what a gift it is that God came into the world to be with you as you are, where you are, so that you would know that you do not have to be perfect or powerful to experience the saving grace of God. The good news of Christmas, the good news of the Gospel is that God knows what life is like, and is with us every step of the way, loving us, guiding us, and saving us. I call this little story, "Once in Woodrow Wilson Service Station."

******

The weather forecast had predicted that the snow storm might be the storm of the century. "Snowmaggedon" the newscasters were calling it, as they urged everyone on the East Coast to batten down the hatches. "They always do this" Jay said to his girlfriend, Meredith, as they watched T.V. "They are just looking for news to fill their 24-hour news cycle. After all this hype, you just watch, the storm will completely miss us, or end up producing little more than a 1/4 of an inch; you'll see." But enough people were listening to the hype that by the next day, the grocery store shelves were picked cleaned of milk, bottled water, bundled firewood, batteries and toilet paper. "Just how long do people think they are going to have to stay home?" Jay wondered as he waited in a line that wrapped completely around the full circumference of the Safeway. By the third day of predictions and panic, however, the hype started getting to him too. "If we're going to make it to your mothers before the storm, we better leave tomorrow instead of waiting for the weekend as we originally planned" he told Meredith. "I'm sure that if we leave in the morning, we'll be way ahead of the storm."

Unfortunately, they were not the only people who had thought to outrun the weather. By the time they finally made it past the Delaware Memorial Bridge and onto the New Jersey turnpike on their way north to New York, the traffic had slowed to a stand-still. Jay tried to keep the atmosphere in the car light, cranking up the radio and cracking a lot of jokes. But when they had moved only a half mile in an hour, and the flurries started coming down in earnest, both he and Meredith agreed that they needed to stop. Meredith was 8 1/2 months pregnant with the couple's first child, which is why they were heading to her mother's. This baby was a surprise to them both. They weren't sure they were ready for it individually or as a couple. So, they wanted the baby to be born where family could help, while they figured out what their future should be. But now Meredith just looked uncomfortable and anxious. Even if there had been no traffic, they would have had hours of driving ahead of them. So, when they finally inched their way to an exit for a rest stop, they pulled off the highway.

Walking into the Woodrow Wilson Service Station, they were instantly hit with the aroma of Roy Rodgers fried chicken and Starbucks coffee, mixed with wet and stressed humanity, way too much humanity. The place was a zoo. While the piped-in radio blasted *"Welcome to the Hotel California,"* families with screaming children crowded around too-small tables. Tourists from who-knows-where shopped and milled about; Meredith heard Korean, Spanish, and something eastern European – maybe Polish? -- as she carefully tiptoed around a couple of homeless people, who had also come inside to avoid the storm, to join a few dozen other women in line for the bathroom. The local vendors were trying their best to take advantage of the crowds, hawking over-priced windshield wiper fluid and ice scrapers and snow globes, along with the usual rhinestone-encrusted smart phone covers and designer sun glasses. While he waited for Meredith, Jay walked over to get some coffee. A teenage girl with dyed black hair and an impressive number of painful looking piercings, stared at him wearily through heavily made-up eyes as she gave him his change. After waiting in line forever for the bathroom, Meredith returned to the main room and found Jay sitting like a homeless person himself on the floor against the wall in the corner, checking on the path of the storm on his phone. There were no chairs left anywhere. "I really don't feel very good" she said. Jay looked concerned. She wasn't supposed to be due for another couple of weeks. But a half an hour later it became clear that whether it was convenient or not the baby had his own sense of timing and was on his way. When Jay called 911, the operator told him that the roads were already so bad and there had been so many accidents that she did not know when an ambulance could get there. They needed to accept that they might have to do the delivery on their own.

Trying to remain calm, the couple headed over to the information booth and told the man staffing it what was going on. Alarmed, the man told them that all he had to offer them was a first aid kit and an emergency defibrillator. There were no medical professionals on staff at the plaza, "liability reasons, you know." He paged the crowd seeking a doctor, but no one stepped forward, probably because everyone was too preoccupied with their own troubles to pay attention to the announcement or respond. "I'm afraid the only place that I can offer you for the birth which is even vaguely private is the employee lounge off a hallway next to the Starbucks" the man told them. So, Jay and Meredith worked their way through the crowds to the sad little room, which smelled of stale cigarette smoke, and was furnished with only a small metal table, a noisy vending machine, and an orange vinyl couch with a tear on one cushion. Meredith groaned, brushed a half-eaten bag of pork rinds off the couch, curled up and closed her eyes.

Michael, a homeless man camped out in the hallway near the lounge, was the first to hear the cry of the baby when he arrived. Michael's hair was unwashed and wild, and his clothes were dirty; but when he peeked around the door and took stock of the situation, his face softened and his eyes grew bright. "Here" he said to the couple. "Take my paper. Newspaper is sterile ya' know." Then he quickly shuffled out of the room, returning a few moments later with one of the cleaning crew at the plaza, Elena, from El Salvador. She smiled, offered prayer in Spanish, and then quickly set about cleaning and disinfecting the room. They were soon joined by the Goth girl from the Starbucks who had come to the room on her break. "Whoa-- a baby!" she said, "Cool." Whipping out her phone, she took a picture of the new family and immediately started texting. Soon the woman she was texting, one of the staff who worked in the mini-mart, came running into the room, carrying a travel-size package of Pampers, a bottle of milk, and a tiny t-shirt which said, "I ♥ New Jersey" on it for the baby. With her was the man from the information booth, who looked both relieved and unexpectedly teary-eyed after seeing the baby. He pulled himself together and extended congratulations, along with some Pizza Hut gift certificates for the family. A few minutes after that, a heavy-set, 60-something security guard came in. He gently placed a little stuffed lion, also from the gift shop, next to the baby, and assured Meredith that he would be watching for the paramedics and would bring them in as soon as the ambulance arrived.

As the piped-in music blared *"We Are Family"*, the irritable crowd outside the lounge continued to shop and grouse about the weather, oblivious to the additional soul who had joined them in the lounge next door. But for those inside the lounge taking turns holding the baby, everything had changed. The snow, the stress, even their own circumstances didn't seem to matter so much in that moment. They were utterly captivated by the new life before them. He made them reflect on their own lives, on love, loss and dreams yet to be fulfilled. In his newness and vulnerability, he made them want to be better people. Jay and Meredith looked at each other and knew that whatever it might hold, their future was together with him. As they gazed into his eyes, they tried to imagine what kind of man this baby, who was already so fond of surprises, would one day grow to be. Whoever he became, everyone there knew that they would never forget his arrival, and that when they returned to their own homes, they would not be the same people they were before.

May the God of peace fill you with all joy and peace in believing, so that you abound in joy and hope for the glory of God, this day and every day. Amen.

When God is Silent
Psalm 42; Matthew 27: 46-50

Last week one of our scripture lessons was the parable of the widow and the unjust judge. (Luke 18:1-8). I said that it was a parable which teaches us about the importance of working persistently for justice for "the least of these," which is true. But often, that parable is interpreted as a lesson on the importance of being persistent in prayer. "Keep on praying," preachers say, "just like the widow, and God who is just and good will not tarry to grant you what you seek." Luke sets the parable up as a lesson on prayer, so I understand why the passage is used that way; prayer is an essential part of discipleship. The only problem with using the parable this way to teach this lesson, however, is that prayer doesn't seem to work that way in the real world. History is filled with examples of people who prayed persistently and did not get justice or whatever else they asked for, at least not in this lifetime. Maybe your own life history is filled with examples too. The hard and confusing reality of faith in the real world is that people do not always get what they pray for, even if they are good, faithful, persistent-in-prayer people. The reality is that often when people pray, what they hear afterwards is silence, lots and lots of divine silence. So, today's "Faith and the Real World" question is: "What do you do when God is silent?"

In my experience, there are at least two different kinds of divine silence that give us pause. One kind is experienced by people who, much of the time, have a strong connection with God. This is a silence that feels like abandonment because it's such a change from the norm. You think you know and understand God. You think you are being faithful and are in touch with the Spirit. You are doing good things for God in the world and then bam! Something bad happens, and right when you most need to discern a word from the Lord, or to feel God's comforting presence, despite praying more than ever, all you feel is empty space, and all you hear is... crickets. You can't even tell if this means God is saying "no" to your prayers, or if God is simply "out to lunch" and indifferent to your suffering. All you know is the silence is deafening.

The other kind of silence is experienced by people who have not yet discovered how God is with them and speaking to them. There are people who long to know God – you may be one of them-- who despite their best efforts never hear or experience anything which seems to confirm in their souls that God is real. They know the stories of how God talked to Moses from a burning bush, and how some people have had other dramatic encounters with the divine. They have heard their friends talk about feeling God in all kinds of ways. But they have never personally experienced either a booming voice or a "still, small" one. They have never felt a moment when they could tell beyond a shadow of a doubt that the God we read about and talk about so much knows them, cares for them, and is somehow in contact reaching out trying to communicate with them.

Both kinds of silences can feel lousy and fill you with longing; as the ancient song writer, the Psalmist, put it in today's text: "As a deer longs for flowing streams, so my soul longs for you.... My tears have been my food day and night, while people say to me continually, 'Where is your God?'" Both kinds of silence can fill you with frustration and despair too, as modern song writer Richard Mullins put it in his song *"Hard to Get."* Mullins sings:

You who live in heaven,
Hear the prayers of those of us who live on earth, Who are afraid of being left by those we love And who get hardened by the hurt.
Do you remember when you lived down here where we all scraped To find the faith to ask for daily bread?
Did you forget about us after you had flown away?
While I memorized every word you said.
Still I'm so scared, I'm holding my breath, While you're up there just playing hard to get.[94]

Most people feel like this at least once in their lives. But despite what it feels like, if there is one thing that Scripture affirms beyond the shadow of a doubt, it is that our God, Yahweh, is not "hard to get," in the sense of being hard to reach --just the opposite. Psalm 139 reminds us that there is nowhere we can ever go, not even to the

---

[94] HARD TO GET, Richard Mullins ©Liturgy Legacy Music and Word Music, LLC (Both admin. By WB Music Corp.). All Rights Reserved. (Used with permission.)

land of the dead to get away from God. (Ps. 139:7-12). Jesus said that his kingdom was within us, and that he would be with us always, even until the end of the age. (Luke 17:20-21; Matt. 28:20). Paul said that we live and move and have our being in God. (Act 17:28). From the story of Adam and Eve to the story of the New Jerusalem in the end of time, the Bible affirms consistently and overwhelmingly that our God is very much with us always, knows us better than we know ourselves, and loves us more than we will ever realize in this lifetime. We can't shake God from our side even if we want to; so, we need never fear that God is a distant watchmaker or simply out to lunch.

We do need to recognize, however, that our God is "hard to get" in the sense that God will be forever beyond our understanding. We will never know in this life why God does not intervene to prevent human suffering, or at least make humanity's blessings and pain equitably distributed. We will never fully understand why God says "no" to life-or-death prayers offered by good people on behalf of their loved ones. We will never know why God has chosen throughout the ages to speak to some individuals in very dramatic ways, but not to everyone this way. We cannot "get" God like we can "get" fellow human beings; and we certainly cannot control God. What we can "get," if we study Scripture and human history, pray fervently and listen carefully, however, is a better understanding of the fact that God speaks to us not just through thunderstorms, burning bushes and booming voices from the sky, but also in silence. Knowing this can make all the difference in our trying to be faithful during it.

Maybe we do not affirm that truth enough in the Church. We all like the theophany stories where God is so present in such dramatic, even scary ways, that it knocks people's socks off. So, we teach our children about Moses' bush, and about how some disciples saw Jesus transformed on a mountaintop. But we do not spend as much time studying the stories about people's spiritual droughts, or emphasizing the stories in which God seems to be absent, like the in the story of Esther. God's name is not mentioned once in that book! Even in the stories in which God does speak there are great chunks of silence. Remember that the reason Abraham and Sarah went ahead and had Ishmael through Hagar, is that after God's voice told them to leave everything they knew to go into a new land to become the ancestors of a whole new people, they then had to endure "radio silence" for years. Imagine them wandering as octogenarians through a new land filled with wonders and dangers, waiting to have a miraculous baby, crying "Marco, Marco?" but never hearing a divine "Polo" for years to guide them. Remember also the scripture lesson the kids picked for Youth Sunday a few weeks ago about the call of Samuel. It began with the phrase, "the Word of the Lord was rare in those days." (1 Sam. 3:1) It was so rare that the head priest, Eli, didn't even recognize God's voice at first when God spoke to Samuel. Even God's chosen ministers in the Bible endure silence.

The truth is that you can't get through this human existence without experiencing the silence of God, which is why Jesus himself cried out from the cross, "My God, my God why have you forsaken me." He had prayed until he was sweating blood in the garden that he wouldn't have to be crucified. But God did not answer that prayer in the way he wanted. So, Luke says that when Jesus was crucified, he cried out in abandonment quoting the beginning of the 22nd Psalm. But in the *Gospel of John*, Jesus cries out "I'm thirsty" just like the deer in today's psalm. His soul was thirsty not for wine or vinegar, but for God. The human Jesus of Nazareth knew just as well as we how hard, scary, and frustrating it is when we cannot hear or feel God, and when God doesn't grant our prayers. He needed to feel that, or no one would have ever believed that he was truly human, let alone believed that he was God.

When God is silent, creation does the talking for God. Sometimes when God is silent, some of God's people speak for God. So, we need to modify our expectations of how God speaks. We also need to recognize that sometimes the best way for God to convey how much God loves us after not granting our prayers is by not saying a word.

When I was a seminary intern at a church in New Jersey, one of the things I did was to mentor a confirmand named Elizabeth. She was sweet, bright, and talented. Anyone would have loved to be her mentor, but the reason I was assigned to her was that her father had just died, as a relatively young man, of cancer. So, I was assigned to her on the theory that my seminary education would help me field tough theological questions about God, if she had them. She didn't. We baked cookies and went for walks and talking about the saving and sustaining power of God. It was great. Then not long after she was confirmed, Elizabeth herself was diagnosed with cancer, an aggressive form of leukemia. She braved her way through all kinds of horrible treatment on both coasts of the U.S., but she didn't make it. I think she was about fifteen when she died.

Now I ask you this, what on earth could I or the pastor have possibly said to her mother, who lost both her husband and her daughter prematurely, and in such a short period? Any words I said would have been at best clichéd pablum and at worst an insult to her pain. That is why one of the first things students are taught in seminary is that sometimes the best pastoral care a person can offer is to sit with someone in silence. You just sit with them so they will know that they are not alone, that they are loved, and that you will weep when they weep and rage when they rage. I think that in the worst situations when God does not answer our prayers, for reasons beyond our understanding, the silence we hear after our loss is God's way of being pastoral. What reason could God give that would take the pain away? Even if God said, "Your loved one had to die, or you have to die to save the world" I don't think we would feel comforted. The loss would still be there; and God's reason would just make us want to ask why it had to be that way. So instead of offering explanations, God crawls into the bed of grief with us, and is silent.

For those who are tormented by the other kind of silence, the kind that comes from not feeling that God is real, the psalmist gives us a clue about how to navigate. Back and forth throughout Psalm 42 the author swings from the pain of the silence to the joy of being in the faith community. The liturgy and music, the opportunities to serve as a leader and to hear the stories of all God has done all help remind and reassure the author of the loving presence of God. It's like the old story of the person who came to a pastor and said, "I can't say the Affirmation of Faith because I don't believe all that is in it." The pastor said, "Keep on saying it until you do." He wasn't trying to suggest brainwashing or spiritual hypocrisy. The pastor was trying to convey that sometimes the best way to find God is to live as one who knows and walks with God. By surrounding yourself with believers, by doing what you are called to do, you surround yourself with "evidence" of the reality of God. You allow God's creation and creatures to speak for Christ, until in the silence, you can hear Christ walking beside you on your own.

When I was in college, one of my roommates chose to do her senior thesis on the works of a certain playwright. "Oh" I said when I first learned of her topic choice. "What about his plays are you going to be writing? His characters? His plots? Certain themes?" "None of that" she said. "I am going to focus on where he puts pauses." At the time, I was completely bewildered by that choice. "You're writing about where he doesn't write? A whole thesis on commas and empty space?" But now I do. Silence can convey volumes. We tend to think of it as conveying only anger or indifference or absence. But it can convey love and intimacy too, when we let it. This is what Elijah felt after he ran away from his ministry. He didn't hear God speaking to his heart in a big, dramatic storm; he heard and felt God's love in the silence that followed. (1 Kings 19:12). In a similar way to how a longtime married couple can feel connected and loved sitting together in a room without talking, God's silence speaks to us of how well God knows us, and how much God loves us. We just need to change how we see and hear the pauses.

There's a story about a farmer who came to visit a friend in New York City for the first time that conveys this well. Walking near Time Square one day, the farm boy suddenly remarked, "I hear a cricket." "You're crazy," his city friend replied, "It's the noon rush hour, and in all of this traffic noise you heard a cricket? C'mon man!" "No, I did hear a cricket," the visitor insisted. Focusing more intently, he walked to the corner, crossed the busy avenue, and looked all around. Finally, he approached a shrub in a large cement planter. Digging beneath the cover mulch he found his cricket. His friend couldn't believe what he had seen. But the friend from the farm said, "My ears are no different from yours. It simply depends on what you have learned to listen for. Here, let me show you." He then reached into his pants pocket, pulled out a handful of change, and dropped the coins on the sidewalk. At the sound of the money hitting the pavement, every head along the crowded block turned. "You see what I mean?" the visitor said. "It all depends on what you are listening for."[95]

---

[95] Shelby, Donald J., "*Hear Here!*", Sept. 8, 1991, Santa Monica, California, 1-2, as cited in Animating Illustrations, "Listening", HOMILETICSONLINE.COM, retrieved at http://www.homilecticsonline.com. (Used with permission.)

Sometimes hearing crickets is a good thing. Next time you are hearing them instead of a dramatic word from the Lord, trust and believe that God is with you in the silence, and listen for the assurance of God's grace and love. Whether your prayers are answered, you can be sure that both the assurance and God are there. Thanks be to God. Amen.

www.ingramcontent.com/pod-product-compliance
Lightning Source LLC
Chambersburg PA
CBHW071517080526
44588CB00011B/1466